Presented To:

_____

From:

_____

Date:

_____

THE
PRAYER
FROM THE
CRYPT

Destiny Image Books by Hank Kunneman

Barrier Breakers

Spiritual A.D.D.

THE
PRAYER
FROM THE
CRYPT

Keys to Reaching the Souls
of Your Loved Ones and Others

HANK KUNNEMAN

DESTINY IMAGE® PUBLISHERS, INC.

P.O. Box 310, Shippensburg, PA 17257-0310

"Promoting Inspired Lives."

This book and all other Destiny Image, Revival Press, MercyPlace, Fresh Bread, Destiny Image Fiction, and Treasure House books are available at Christian bookstores and distributors worldwide.

For a U.S. bookstore nearest you, call **1-800-722-6774.**

For more information on foreign distributors, call **717-532-3040.**

Reach us on the Internet: **www.destinyimage.com.**

ISBN 13 TP: 978-0-7684-0304-6

ISBN 13 Ebook: 978-0-7684-8782-4

For Worldwide Distribution, Printed in the U.S.A.

1 2 3 4 5 6 7 8 / 16 15 14 13 12

ENDORSEMENT

Hank Kunneman is a man after God's own heart. He operates in the prophetic, pastors with passion, and practices what he preaches. Thank you, Hank, for proclaiming Jesus Christ to be the spotless Lamb of God, crucified, risen, and victorious.

Within these pages you will find practical tools that explain the *whys and hows* of witnessing. These chapters will help stir the heart and awaken a fresh burden for lost family members, friends, and neighbors. May these principles open our eyes to see and to feel a greater burden for the lost, not just our immediate family but those in our sphere of influence and beyond.

Steve Hill
Pastor, Evangelist

[Jesus said], "There was a rich man who was dressed in purple and fine linen and lived in luxury every day. At his gate was laid a beggar named Lazarus, covered with sores and longing to eat what fell from the rich man's table. Even the dogs came and licked his sores. The time came when the beggar died and the angels carried him to Abraham's side. The rich man also died and was buried. In Hades, where he was in torment, he looked up and saw Abraham far away, with Lazarus by his side. So he called to him, 'Father Abraham, have pity on me and send Lazarus to dip the tip of his finger in water and cool my tongue, because I am in agony in this fire.' But Abraham replied, 'Son, remember that in your lifetime you received your good things, while Lazarus received bad things, but now he is comforted here and you are in agony. And besides all this, between us and you a great chasm has been set in place, so that those who want to go from here to you cannot, nor can anyone cross over from there to us.' He answered, 'Then I beg you, father, send Lazarus to my family, for I have five brothers. Let him warn them, so that they will not also come to this place of torment.' Abraham replied, 'They have Moses and the Prophets; let them listen to them.' 'No, father Abraham,' he said, 'but if someone from the dead goes to them, they will repent.' He said to him, 'If they do not listen to Moses and the Prophets, they will not be convinced even if someone rises from the dead'" (Luke 16:19-31 NIV).

CONTENTS

Chapter One

THE REQUEST FROM HELL

Then he said, I pray thee therefore, father, that thou wouldest send him to my father's house: for I have five brethren; that he may testify unto them, lest they also come into this place of torment (Luke 16:27-28).

The heat was unbearable, and the flames burned with unquench-able pain. Before he died, this man had everything—the finest clothes, the best possessions, and great wealth. After being placed in the crypt, he found himself in hell and there was nothing that this rich man could do. He was full of pain, agony, and torments inde-scribable—nothing could alleviate the suffering. His cry for mercy would fall on deaf ears; not even the smallest taste of cool water could be brought to him for a moment of relief.

In the never-ending pain of his despair, he cried out repeatedly for help; he had a request so urgent, so important that he pleaded unceasingly from his prison of misery. What was his request? Noth-ing else but that a man might be allowed to go and warn his five brothers so that they may not find themselves in the hell he was experiencing. It was truly one man's desperate plea to save his family.

THE PRAYER FROM DOWN UNDER

These details describe a parable that Jesus tells in Luke 16 of two men who die. The first man is named Lazarus, a beggar who died and was carried by the angels into Paradise. The other man, a rich man, was buried in a crypt and is seen in hell describing the horror of his suffering. He is in agony, thirsty, tormented in a flame, and crying for mercy. He has full use of his senses, emotions, and faculties. He is able to express his desires. He lifts up his voice with a prayer from hell. However, his prayer is not to the Lord but to Father Abraham who he sees afar off in Paradise.

Think for a moment of all the things he might request.

The rich man begs for something that should send shivers down our spines. He asks that Lazarus would be allowed to go warn his five brothers not to come to this place where he is without hope, without

God, without relief, and lost forever. The deepest desire he had in his soul was for his family to be warned:

> *Then he said, I pray thee therefore, father, that thou wouldest send him to my father's house: for I have five brethren; that he may testify unto them, lest they also come into this place of torment* (Luke 16:27-28).

He was asking for laborers to go and speak to his relatives. Imagine what people are requesting in hell at this very moment. I guarantee you it is much the same as this rich man. We need to pray for our families to be saved, but we also need to be willing to be used of God to reach other people's families and loved ones.

This story Jesus told reminds me of someone very close to me who died. I will never forget the day I felt the Lord warn me to share the Gospel with him urgently. I had attempted in the past, but to no avail. I tried not to overdo it with him; instead, I would interject the message of salvation from time to time. However, I was feeling stirred from the Lord that I should do this right away, so I went and shared the Gospel with him again. I told him I felt he shouldn't delay to make a true commitment to Jesus and repent of his sin. I can still see the scene as if it was yesterday.

I ministered the Gospel to him, and I could tell this time it was making him think. I decided to ask him right then and there to make a decision because of the seriousness of what I felt. The Gospel of salvation through Jesus was rejected by him once again; he said he wasn't ready for that kind of thing. But this time it was too late. He died a few months later without any evidence of accepting Jesus into his life or making any real lifestyle change. All I know is that God warned me—and warned this loved one. God wanted to reach that person and was counting on me to be a laborer.

I understand that it is possible that he might have called out to Jesus in his last moments. But I certainly won't rule out the fact that he may not be in Heaven because, when a clear opportunity was given, he rejected the Lord. How sad it is that some people will still choose to reject the Lord and harden their hearts no matter who tells them!

> *Abraham saith unto him, They have Moses and the prophets; let them hear them. And he said, Nay, father Abraham: but if one went unto them from the dead, they will repent. And he said unto him, If they hear not Moses and the prophets, neither will they be persuaded, though one rose from the dead* (Luke 16:29-31).

REKINDLE A PASSION FOR PEOPLE

We need to rekindle a passion to reach people with the Gospel, or they will suffer like the man who cried out from hell! Let the following stories ignite a passion for our families as well as for people who don't know the Lord. We must never forget that God has souls on His mind. We need the fire and passion of God for lost humanity to be set on our lips, so we can speak boldly for the Lord. This is what happened to the prophet Isaiah. Once a coal of fire was set on his lips, it was time to go. He responded by saying, "Lord, here am I; send me" (see Isa. 6:6-9). This is true for those of us who love the Lord as well. We need to allow the fire of God's passion and love to ignite our lives so that we too will be willing to go and share the Gospel of Jesus Christ!

This was also the case after tongues of fire settled upon those in the Upper Room in Acts 2. That fire of the Holy Ghost burned so strongly in the disciples and others gathered there that thousands turned to the Lord as a result. I understand that sometimes we lack the fire and passion to reach people, but we can't excuse ourselves; we still have to reach them and tell them of the wonders of Heaven and the tragedies of hell.

Years ago, I tried to reach a certain co-worker for Jesus. I have always tried to stay on fire for God and passionate about reaching souls, but he was the greatest challenge to sharing the Gospel I had ever faced. I always did my best to do my job; after all, that was why I was hired. Yet, when you are full of the Holy Ghost and His fire is in you, it is hard to hide it. I didn't need to use valuable work time to share the Gospel because people could see it; some liked it, and others hated it. This man, "Lance," hated it, despising the Gospel. He was very vocal about it, and set himself to make my life miserable every day at work. It was hard to have a passion to reach him or even share the Gospel with him. This can be especially true when people are mean and persecute you or resist the Gospel.

Lance would have fits of rage with me even when I wasn't talking about the Lord. He would get in my face and mock God and my Christianity. I was a young Christian and didn't respond by being aggressive. I was always told that Jesus said to turn the other cheek, so that is what I did. Lance would arrive at work a few minutes after I opened the business. He did this because no one else was around; he would drink his coffee hung-over from the night before, yelling at me about the Gospel. I wouldn't even bring it up, but my mere presence was enough to stir up his legion of demons. This man was tormented, and it was evident. Lance was in his mid-forties but looked like he was in his late sixties due to his lifestyle. That didn't surprise me because the Bible says the way of the sinner is hard (see Prov. 13:15).

One time I had put my Bible on top of my car while I was getting ready to leave. Lance grabbed my Bible, waved it wildly in the air, and threw it to the ground. He then stomped on it in pure rage against God. He told me that he once physically removed a pastor who came to his home to pray for him. He would deny the reality of hell or Heaven by saying that when he died he would be buried six feet under and push up daisies. It seemed the more I prayed for him the worse he became and the more he persecuted me. It was very difficult to have a passion to reach him.

Unfortunately, this story has a tragic ending. About a year after I left that job to pursue ministry, I heard that Lance had died. He committed suicide by putting a gun to his head. It hurt me greatly to hear the news because I wanted to reach him and had tried so desperately. The last anyone knew he died an angry man, bitter, resistant, and continuing to curse and reject Jesus. I pray somehow he called out to the Lord. If not, he too may be as the rich man—remembering the days the Gospel was presented to him and crying out for someone to reach his family.

THE CHAMBER OF HELL IS WIDE OPEN

Literally speaking, a crypt is a holding chamber used for the burial of a corpse that in ancient times was used for the burial of important religious and political figures. Today however, it has become a chilling symbol of the finality of death, especially for those who are lost without Christ. They see the crypt as a message that speaks to their lost state. We know this is true as Hollywood and novel writers show the horrors of hell simultaneously with the crypt; and the word *crypt* is used to speak of death, demons, and encounters with evil. To most it represents what it means to be lost in a state of haunting torment called hell.

Hell is real, and you may have heard some say in jest that "people are dying to get in." The Bible says that hell has a wide mouth that swallows those who reject Jesus and die without knowing Him (see Isa. 5:14). Sadly, at this very second, hell is receiving the lost souls of men and women; yet, according to this verse, it never gets full. It just enlarges itself with more and more unsaved people. The Bible also says that *"Hell and destruction are never full"* (Prov. 27:20)!

Don't believe the lie that is circulating throughout the earth today—even in some churches—that hell isn't real. It is most certainly real, and Jesus made reference to it many times in Scripture, even speaking more of hell than Heaven. Jesus emphasized the reality of hell because He doesn't want people to go there—He loves the souls of men and women.

It is not popular to talk or preach about hell, but it needs to be done. The devil himself knows it is a real place and has gone overboard to convince people it doesn't exist. Think of how often people use the word *hell* as a curse word, thinking nothing of whether it is a literal place or their current destination. In fact, the devil loves when people make light of hell, as though it will be a picnic with deviled eggs, deviled ham, and that oh-so-famous devil's food cake. In all seriousness, it is not going to be a joyful picnic. There have been many debates and discussion, and much dismissing of hell. I believe it is an attempt to excuse our sinful behavior and ignore God's righteous judgment. Satan loves to get people to think hell is nonexistent.

What is hell? Hell is a spiritual location in the middle of this earth. How do we know this? Jesus mentioned it as He was speaking of His death and resurrection:

> *For as Jonas was three days and three nights in the whale's belly; so shall the Son of man be three days and three nights in the heart of the earth* (Matthew 12:40).

There is nothing that would remotely represent paradise in the belly of a whale. I believe Jesus was comparing hell to the horrific experience Jonah encountered in the belly of the whale, a hellish experience deep within. He was saying that the time Jonah spent in the belly of the whale was a type of the experience Jesus would have in the heart of the earth while redeeming the souls of lost men and women.

Hell is the place where the vengeance of God is visited upon those who do not know God: *"In flaming fire taking vengeance on them that know not God, and that obey not the gospel of our Lord Jesus Christ"* (2 Thess. 1:8). It is also the place where those who reject God as their Savior and Lord are punished: *"Who shall be punished with everlasting destruction from the presence of the Lord, and from the glory of his power"* (2 Thess. 1:9).

Jesus, when speaking to the scribes and Pharisees, spoke of hell as a real location: *"Serpents, brood of vipers! How can you escape the condemnation of hell?"* (see Matt. 23:33). He wasn't speaking symbolically as some would suggest but warning them of a literal place in which some would be condemned without accepting Jesus as their Lord. When we study different meanings for the word *hell* in Scripture, we find words like *Gehenna*, *Hades*, and *Sheol*. In the Gospels, two of these words, *Gehenna* and *Hades* (Greek words translated as "hell"), are used. In the story of the rich man and Lazarus the beggar, the Greek word *Hades* is used for the location of this rich man: *"...the rich man also died, and was buried; and in hell he lift up his eyes, being in torments..."* (Luke 16:22-23).

Again, this place is in the belly of the earth where the souls of lost people are until the final judgment when the lake of fire will encompass the different parts of hell, including Hades. Hell, or the lake of fire, is the final place where the lost souls of men and women, as well as Satan, demons, and fallen angels, will be for all eternity. It is the final hell for those who have rejected the Lord. We must realize that once a person is in hell, he or she will always be in hell. This isn't a temporary holding place from which people can work their way up into Heaven; it is a permanent place of torment. In this terrible place, they can't be let out, bought out, prayed out, or in any other way freed.

Often, when Jesus spoke about hell, the word He used is translated in the Greek as *Gehenna*. There are some theological debates regarding this word that cause some scholars to reject the idea of a literal hell. Some say Jesus was using this word *Gehenna* only to refer to a literal, physical valley outside Jerusalem mentioned in the Hebrew Bible as the Valley of the Son of Hinnom. They suggest that this place only referred to that garbage dump outside of Jerusalem and not to a literal place of suffering called hell.

However, those who were listening to Jesus knew exactly what He was referring to and why He was comparing hell to a literal garbage dump. Jesus was using these words (*Gehenna, Hades*) to describe a physical place called hell. In other words, He used a natural example to illustrate a spiritual (and, in this case, physical) reality. For example, when Jesus gave an illustration with regard to prayer and faith, He pointed to a physical mountain to make a spiritual application: *"For verily I say unto you, That whosoever shall say unto this mountain, Be thou removed, and be thou cast into the sea..."* (Mark 11:23). Notice Jesus said "this" mountain, meaning a literal mountain. Many may argue about hell and its definitions, yet one thing remains. Jesus said, *"And these will go away into eternal punishment: but the righteous into life eternal"* (Matt. 25:46 NASB).

This place called hell is real enough for Jesus, as we mentioned before, to tell us of the rich man who suffered there and begged that his family be saved. The Bible gives us some insight into this horrific place. As we read this story of the rich man, we can see that Jesus pointed out two separate, literal places, one being paradise and the other hell: *"...the beggar died, and was carried by the angels into*

Abraham's bosom: the rich man also died, and was buried; and in hell he lift up his eyes" (Luke 16:22-23). If you believe in Paradise, then you have to believe in hell because the Lord referred to both.

We can also see from this story that this rich man was very aware of his horrible surroundings: he could feel pain; he could talk, see, and feel. He was in agony and torments:

> *And in hell he lift up his eyes, **being in torments,** and seeth Abraham afar off, and Lazarus in his bosom. And he cried and said, Father Abraham, have mercy on me, and send Lazarus, that he may dip the tip of his finger in water, and cool my tongue; for I am tormented in this flame* (Luke 16:23-24).

Notice in these verses the Bible says the man was in torments, plural. This means more than one kind of torment and at more than one time! This man in hell was very much alive even though he was lost, in the sense that his spirit, which is eternal, never dies. As a result, he was desperate for even a degree of relief from his torments, but couldn't receive it because he was eternally lost and separated from God. Another alarming thing we see is that hell is a place where people scream and beg for mercy as they are tormented in its fire (see Luke 16:23-24). And it is a place where many pray but receive no relief or answer to their prayers. They beg for relief or for someone to warn their loved ones not to come to this place! (See Luke 16:24-28.)

Let's look at a few descriptions of what hell is like:

1. It is a literal place (see Matt. 23:33).

2. It has an unquenchable fire that never goes out (see Matt. 5:22, Mark 9:43).

3. It is a place into which the wicked will be thrown (see Matt. 5:29-30).

4. It is the outer darkness, a blackness that lasts forever (see Matt. 8:12, Jude 13).

5. It is a place of weeping and gnashing of teeth (see Matt. 8:12, 22:13, 25:30).

6. Hell is real and was not created or meant for humankind (see Matt. 25:41).

7. Hell is the place where "their worm dieth not" (Mark 9:44).

8. It is a place of eternal torments (see Luke 16:23; Rev. 14:10-11).

9. Men gnaw their tongues because of pain and curse God here (see Rev. 16:10-11).

10. It is a bottomless pit and lake of fire (see Rev. 9:1; 19:20).

As we look at this list, we can certainly see that no one with any sanity would want to go there. In fact, I am convinced people don't have the capacity to comprehend fully what hell and its torments are like without the Holy Spirit revealing it through a spiritual revelation or experience. If we were to experience such a thing we wouldn't be able to function, think, live, or speak! Hell is an awful place that was never intended for humankind. What is more tragic is that, according to Scripture, many more will go to hell than Heaven (see Matt. 7:13-14).

FEW BE THAT FIND IT

It is imperative we understand not only the reality of hell, but the seriousness of it—souls once there are lost forever! The devil wants nothing more than to lure, invite, and deceive so that as many people as possible end up with him in that dreadful place called hell. He not only tries to convince people that hell isn't real; he also tries to get people to think that more people are going to Heaven than to hell. He encourages them to dismiss their carnal, fleshly, compromising behavior with lies such as, "Well, I'm a good person. I don't do anything bad"; "I go to church"; or "I'm a [particular religion], and it is the same God. As long as I am good and believe, I will go to Heaven." This couldn't be further from the truth because Scripture tells us that we have all sinned, and not one of us is righteous on our own (see Rom. 3:23). It doesn't matter who you are or what you have done, good or bad. We all need to repent of our sins and come to God by the only way available, through Jesus: *"Jesus saith unto him, I am the way, the truth, and the life: no man cometh unto the Father, but by me"* (John 14:6).

Scripture reveals that the majority of people are on a wide road leading to hell (see Matt. 7:13-14). Sadly, one day I heard a preacher say just the opposite. This is not what Jesus taught! He taught that few were on the *narrow* road to Heaven. This means, according to Jesus, that more are in hell than in Heaven. You might be saying, "How can that be?" Obviously nobody knows the ultimate numbers, but God alone. Yet, Jesus gave us some things we need to consider regarding the ratio of those who are saved to those who are not. Let me show you a few examples that highlight the seriousness of reaching our families and other people with the Gospel.

Jesus Himself said that not everyone who says to Him, "Lord, Lord," will enter into the Kingdom of Heaven (see Matt. 7:21). He mentions this after explaining that more are on the wide road that leads to destruction than on the narrow road that leads to life:

> *You can enter God's Kingdom only through the narrow gate. The highway to hell is broad, and its gate is wide for the many who choose that way. But the gateway to life is very narrow and the road is difficult, and only a few ever find it* (Matthew 7:13-14 NLT).

Do you notice that the road to hell is broad because more travel on that road than on the narrow road to Heaven?

Another example we find is in Mark 4; in this parable, Jesus speaks of a sower who sows the Word of God into the hearts of men and women. Three out of the four soils (speaking of hearts) in this story weren't considered good ground. But one ground yielded thirty, sixty, and one hundred fold. According to this parable, if we were to consider the ratio of those who receive the Word of God with those who don't, we would find that the majority didn't receive. This may mean that only about 25 percent of those who have the Gospel shared with them receive it.

Then we can't forget that there were only eight people saved in the flood of Noah compared to the rest of the world who died because they rejected God and chose not to heed Noah's warnings. The Bible refers to Noah's family as the few who were saved—versus the many who were disobedient and died:

> *Which sometime were disobedient, when once the long-suffering of God waited in the days of Noah, while the ark was a preparing, wherein few, that is, eight souls were saved by water* (1 Peter 3:20).

And let's not forget Abraham's family and the few in his nephew Lot's family who escaped Sodom and Gomorrah's destruction (see Gen. 19:24-30).

From all of these examples, we can see that the majority of people born in this earth may not make it to Heaven. This should help us to imagine the number of cries and the pleas coming from hell for relief and for someone to warn loved ones not to come there. *We* **cannot** *be asleep in the harvest.* We have to reach as many as we can, for the Lord, so people can be saved.

If the majority of people may not make it to Heaven, then we all the more need true conversions and not just decisions. True conversions involve more than just counting how many pray the sinner's prayer; true conversions produce true disciples. In today's church trends, preachers often stand up to give a call for salvation (which they should) and then boast of the number who prayed the sinner's prayer. This is great, except that these same people may not be accounted for again; they fall through the cracks. In other churches, we find that the people attending aren't given an opportunity to get saved and commit their lives to the Lord. And in yet other churches, it has become a trend to believe that anyone who prays a prayer is automatically saved, regardless of whether any fruit of a true Christian life follows. The mindset is that if you made the decision to be saved, you are going to Heaven and your lifestyle cannot jeopardize that salvation.

I believe a large part of the problem occurs after the prayer of salvation. People are left to disciple themselves in the things of the Lord without mentors, a standard of righteousness, or a model of radical Christian living to follow. God wants conversion; He said that unless you are converted, you can't inherit the kingdom of Heaven (see Matt. 18:3). Conversion means change, a lifestyle change and a truly repentant life, not just the mere repeating of a prayer. Jesus said it even more clearly, "Why do you call Me Lord, but don't do what I say?" (see Luke 6:46). In the Bible, anyone who chose to follow Jesus experienced true conversion and a lifestyle change. The rich man who went to hell never committed his life to the Lord; instead, he chose the things of this world while ignoring his eternal resting place and the needs of others. This is never God's plan—for people to go to hell for all eternity. He never intended for us to make our eternal home in such a place.

Why then do people have to go to this place if God loves them so much?

THE ETERNAL SPIRIT

God does love people, and it is certainly evident in the fact that His own blood was spilled and His body crucified to reconcile us to Himself. It hurts Him that people are tormented in hell at this very moment. It saddens Him that they are crying out for someone to give them relief, just like the rich man, though it's too late. He knows of those who want to cool their tongues and warn their families like the rich man did. Remember, God never intended for any of us to go there, and He doesn't like it, but He doesn't have a choice. The Bible says it was created for the devil and his angels: *"Then shall He say also unto them on the left hand, Depart from me, ye cursed, into everlasting fire, prepared for the devil and his angels"* (Matt. 25:41).

Hell exists because it was originally intended and created for the devil and his angels. However, Adam and Eve sinned and rejected God, so the ultimate penalty for their sin and for the rejection of Jesus is eternal damnation. The only place for a lost eternal soul is in hell with the devil. You see, when someone dies without the Lord and his human spirit isn't reborn, hell becomes the only place where his lost soul can spend eternity. Hell is the place of lost human souls because sin cannot coexist with God; neither can a spirit that has not been reborn enter into Heaven. I know that sounds harsh, but we need to understand God's righteousness and His justice. Sin cannot exist in Heaven, neither can those who reject God—Heaven is without sin and filled only with those who love God and worship Him. God has given us a choice to be saved from our sins through Jesus who paid the price for reconciliation. Once we have accepted Jesus and repented of our sins, our spirits are reborn: *"Jesus answered and said unto him, Verily, verily, I say unto thee, Except a man be born again, he cannot see the kingdom of God"* (John 3:3). This is necessary because when Adam and Eve sinned, it caused all humankind thereafter to die spiritually and physically. You see, we choose to send ourselves to hell by rejecting Jesus as our personal Lord and Savior.

Only through salvation can the human spirit be reborn; only then do we become new creatures in Christ who can live in Heaven (see 2 Cor. 5:17). Simply put, Heaven is filled with those whose spirits have been born anew, and hell is full of those whose spirits are lost and dead without God. Whether we believe it or not, the truth is that no man or woman will stand before God with an excuse:

> *For the invisible things of Him from the creation of the world are clearly seen, being understood by the things that are made, even His eternal power and Godhead; so that they are without excuse* (Romans 1:20).

This means that every person who has ever been born will be without excuse, and our eternal destiny will be fairly determined by God. We may be surprised by those we will find in Heaven and those who did not make it when God separates the sheep (those who followed Him) from the goats (those who didn't) (see Matt. 25).

I cannot say it enough! God doesn't send people to hell; they send themselves. People in hell have chosen to rebel against God;

they are without excuse according to Scripture. Remember, we have a sinful nature and make a choice to sin; after death, the only place for the lost spirits of those who persist in their sin is hell. Let's not forget that God wants people to repent, to change their minds, to believe Him and trust Him:

> For God so loved the world that he gave his only begotten Son, that whosoever believeth in him should not perish, but have everlasting life (John 3:16).

It is not right to accuse God of being heartless, unkind, uncaring, or punitive. He has done everything He can to keep humankind out of hell. Like the lyrics of an old song say, "He gave His life...what more could He give?" It is up to us to choose. He sent His Son to die on the cross for us, to be our sacrifice for sin. He rose from the dead so no one would have to go to that horrific place called hell!

Never think for a moment that God rejoices over lost humanity suffering in hell:

> Say unto them, As I live, saith the Lord GOD, I have no pleasure in the death of the wicked; but that the wicked turn from his way and live... (Ezekiel 33:11).

We must never forget that it was God who first loved us, willing to die for all!

Consider the story of James and John in the book of Luke. They wanted to call down the fire of God and the heat of His wrath to punish a village of Samaritans who would not receive Jesus: "*And when his disciples James and John saw this, they said, Lord, wilt thou that we command fire to come down from heaven, and consume them, even as Elias did?*" (Luke 9:54).

But look at Jesus' response toward their desire to see this village punished:

> He turned, and rebuked them, and said, Ye know not what manner of spirit ye are of. For the Son of man is not come to destroy men's lives, but to save them. And they went to another village (Luke 9:55-56).

Jesus rebuked their desire for God's wrath and informed them that they didn't know what spirit they were operating in. They were not of His Spirit, and they did not yet have His heart for people.

I once asked the Lord why He doesn't eliminate hell altogether, so that no one else has to suffer there—and I believe I heard the Lord put it in perspective for me. God created us in His image; He had to count the cost. He knew we would ultimately sin. Yet, there was something more. If God created us in His own image, God being a Spirit, then that would mean we too would be spirit beings with human shells we call bodies. Why is that important? Well, if God breathes into man the breath of life (see Gen. 2:7), then man becomes a living soul, an eternal spirit being who lives forever. You see, because God breathed His eternal Spirit into us, we will live spiritually forever, and our spirits will go either to Heaven with the Lord or into hell for eternity if we choose to reject Him. God set an angel to guard the Tree of Life for this reason, so that He could protect Adam and Eve from being spiritually lost forever without a chance to be redeemed.

Spirit beings like God, the angels, the devil, demons, and human-kind are eternal, which means they can't cease to exist. If our spirits are not reborn, then we are spiritually lost forever, and the only place lost spirits can go is hell. It was created for the devil and his angels, and God never intended for man to sin and reject Him. Today there are those in hell who will remain in that lost state without hope of redemption! Hell will never cease to exist, and the torment of the lost soul will last forever because hell is an eternal housing for the lost spirits of humankind and demonic spirits. God doesn't want any human being to remain spiritually lost, but to accept Jesus as Lord and Savior and live with Him forever instead!

> *The Lord is not slack concerning his promise, as some men count slackness; but is longsuffering to us-ward, not willing that any should perish, but that all should come to repentance* (2 Peter 3:9).

We need to pray for our loved ones, determined that they will not go to that dreadful place. We must cry out to God for our families and seek to reach them and others for the Lord. Let us not forget, for even a moment, that cry of the rich man in hell: "Lord, please save my family." His cry must become our cry for others while we are alive on this earth. We don't have to be in hell to cry out to no avail; we can cry out here on the earth with results!

Certainly the Gospel is not all hell, fire, and damnation. It contains good news of God's grace, love, and mercy to sinners. Jesus has made the way for us and our families to be with Him forever—to avoid the fate of this rich man, living in hell and crying out for mercy and for his family. God has said that whoever believes, clings to, and trusts in His Son Jesus will not perish but have everlasting life (see John 3:16). Romans 10 makes it clear that if we believe in our hearts that God raised Jesus from the dead and confess Him with our mouths, then we will be saved (see Rom. 10:9-10). Remember, God made the way; whoever calls on the name of the Lord will be saved (Rom. 10:13). He will answer and give the promise of eternal life!

I believe it is not too late to see our families and loved ones turn to the Lord. I also believe it is not too late to change our mindsets concerning lost humanity. In the remaining chapters of this book, I want to show you how you can make a difference. You can reach your family and everyone you meet. I want to encourage you to believe for your whole household to come to know the Lord. What you will discover in the next chapters will ignite your faith to truly believe and see God make a difference in your loved ones' lives!

We need to make our cry like the rich man's request from hell: "Save my family!" Are you ready to learn how? Are you ready to cry out for the salvation of your family and everyone you meet?

Chapter Two

SOMETHING SPECIAL ON GOD'S HEART

In the beginning God created the heavens and the earth.
Now the earth was formless and empty, darkness was
over the surface of the deep, and the Spirit of God was
hovering over the waters. And God said, "Let there be
light," and there was light. God saw that the light was
good... (Genesis 1:1-4 NIV).

If we truly want to rescue lost souls and save our families from that horrible place known as hell, we must first begin by capturing the most special thing upon God's heart, which I do not believe can be fully appreciated unless you tell it as a story that expresses the feeling of God from the very beginning. For a moment let's try to capture God's heart by telling His story.

A word was not yet spoken to bring life and time into existence. Yet One stood, the Three in One, staring into the future, ready to make the greatest decision He would ever make. He was about to bring something into being that would pierce His heart and very being. Standing as one God in three persons, the Father, the Son, and the Holy Spirit knew the seriousness of this decision. It would forever affect the Trinity, humankind, and everything that would be created!

What was the risk of bringing this most treasured desire and longing into being? After all, the Trinity was filled with excitement to bring forth a human race in their image. Humankind would speak to the Lord face to face and love Him in return; yet, there was one thing to consider. If He brought forth the man and woman (see Gen. 5:2) and gave them freedom to choose, would they choose Him or reject Him? Would they make the choice to do wrong and ultimately put a death sentence upon themselves that no one but God could pay?

As you can imagine, this was an extremely important decision and a costly price that would have to be considered if He makes such a man. By choosing to bring Adam and Eve into being, the Godhead was also choosing to provide the necessary propitiation for them and all humankind—because their sin would bring separation. In His foreknowledge and wisdom, He knew all of this, and He knew the ultimate price would have to be paid: the shedding of the blood of the Son of God, Jesus Christ.

THE DECISION BEFORE TIME

Such a mind-staggering thought: God's own blood would be the ultimate price for creating this man and woman. He was willing to create them, though He knew it meant the Son must die for them. His willingness to pay the penalty of our disobedience has never been matched as the greatest act of unselfish love! Just pause and think for a moment of God's amazing love and sacrifice for you and me; creating us meant He must offer His life willingly, shedding His own blood to pay the price for our sins.

Can you imagine what was going on in God's heart as He made this decision before there was time or man and woman? He was willing to proceed with His most treasured delight even though He knew the outcome. What do you suppose He was thinking as He molded the clay from which Adam was made? He had already made the decision that He was willing to die for him. Can you imagine that, as God looked at Adam's lifeless clay body, He knew that He would also take on this very same form one day?

> *So the Word became human and made his home among us. He was full of unfailing love and faithfulness. And we have seen his glory, the glory of the Father's one and only Son* (John 1:14 NLT).

What a sobering thought, that God would offer His own body to be beaten, bloodied, and crucified. What do you think was going on in the Lord's heart as He stared at the lifeless form, His masterpiece, that He held in His hands? He chose to take that beautiful breath of love and breathe His life and being into the clay man named Adam: *"And the LORD God formed man of the dust of the ground, and breathed into his nostrils the breath of life; and man became a living being"* (Gen. 2:7 NKJV). Did God pause before He breathed that precious breath? Did His heart ache the moments before He took such a step of sacrificial love? All we know is that He went forward with His choice. If Jesus endured the cross for the joy set before Him (see Heb. 12:2), I suspect His heart was filled with overflowing joy in these moments too.

What an incredible sight as this clay, molded by God's hand, began to come to life with that breath of sacrificial, intentional love! I can only think of the excitement God must have felt at the moment Adam's heart began to beat. I would give anything to see the expression on God's face and the joy in His heart when He saw Adam's eyes open and heard those precious first words spoken to Him! Wow! Remember, this was all done in the name of love, desire, and craving for fellowship by an all-powerful and loving God. Even in these first moments of Adam's birth, He knew that the price of His own blood for this man and all humankind was imminent. His breath and life were now flowing in Adam, and no one could redeem man and woman from their soon-to-be fallen state but God alone. We must remind ourselves that this was a decision considered by God before time and creation.

How do we know?

We know because Scripture gives us a glimpse of what was taking place before those first creative words of God and the first breath that brought His man to life:

> All who dwell on the earth shall worship Him, whose names have not been written in the Book of Life of the Lamb slain from the foundation of the world (Revelation 13:8 NKJV).

This verse reveals exactly what we have been discussing: Jesus was declared the Lamb slain before the foundation of the world was even created. What does this mean? It means that God the Father, Son, and Holy Ghost discussed, thought about, and finally went forward with their plan to create a man and woman and this world. They did this, knowing it would be filled with the effects of sin and that Jesus would have to come and be crucified like a lamb slaughtered to pay the price of sin. It is the greatest story in all of history. How amazing that God would create man and woman in His image, only for this man and woman to sin and fall short of His glory! *"For all have sinned and come short of the glory of God"* (Rom. 3:23).

As a result, nothing and no one created would be able to pay the ultimate sacrifice and penalty but one alone, Jesus Christ, God's only Son! Most everyone knows the beloved Scripture: *"For God so loved the world that he gave his only begotten Son"* (John 3:16). This reference is often quoted without the full understanding of what actually took place or what is still upon God's heart today: His love and care for people. Before the very foundation of the world, it was agreed upon that God would give His Son Jesus to die for us. This is why we should never doubt God's love or concern for us. He showed the greatest act of caring and love, before we were even born, when He created us knowing He would have to die for us. What an awesome decision—and what an incredible view into God's love for every human soul!

Look at some other verses that reveal that we were on God's heart before time existed:

> *Forasmuch as ye know that ye were not redeemed with corruptible things, as silver and gold, from your vain conversation received by tradition from your fathers; but with the precious blood of Christ, as of a lamb without blemish and without spot:* **who verily was foreordained before the foundation of the world,** *but was manifest in these last times for you* (1 Peter 1:18-20).

Who hath saved us, and called us with an holy calling, not according to our works, but according to his own purpose and grace, **which was given us in Christ Jesus before the world began** (2 Timothy 1:9).

According as **he hath chosen us in him before the foundation of the world,** *that we should be holy and without blame before him in love* (Ephesians 1:4).

When God said, "Let us" make man in our image, He was referring to the *"us"* of the Trinity and to the astonishing decision to create and then be willing to sacrifice all for us. What an amazing grace! This is also why Jesus said, "The work You gave Me I have finished" (see John 17:4). To what work was Jesus referring? I believe He was referring, in part, to the meeting that happened before time, when He agreed to be the one to die for the sins of all humankind. In addition, He was referring to His ministry on earth, which was also foreplanned and determined before humankind was created.

LET THERE BE LIGHT!

On the basis of that heartfelt decision He made before the foundation of the world, it is not difficult to see how important each of us is to God. In fact, the first words spoken by God to create the heavens and the earth were special, revealing a further prophetic glimpse of what was on God's mind. Remember, everything in this earth was created not only for God's pleasure but also with us in mind. God wanted us to enjoy what He had created. For me, the first words uttered by God to bring the process of creation into motion emanate deep love: *"Let there be light!"* (Gen. 1:3).

You might be asking, "How does this relate to us?"

First of all, we know it does because everything created prior to Adam and Eve was made for their participation and enjoyment. Second, we need to observe the prophetic implication of this statement; it does not just speak of natural light that moves approximately 186,000 miles per second, but of a spiritual light that prophetically announces Jesus, God's only begotten Son. He is the one true Light chosen before the foundation of the world. He would come and die for a dark, cold, and sinful world. Do you see it? Let there be Light, or…let there be Jesus! It is a prophetic announcement of Jesus coming to this earth as the spiritual light for all! How do we know that it can apply prophetically to Jesus as that light? Well, the Scripture says that Jesus, when His ministry started, was the Light that people, who sat in spiritual darkness, saw: *"The people who sat in darkness have seen a great light, and upon those who sat in the region and shadow of death Light has dawned"* (Matt. 4:16 NKJV).

"Let there be light" also speaks of Jesus being part of everything that exists in creation. It is a prophetic announcement and message of salvation for a dark and dying world. Jesus, when preaching His famous Sermon on the Mount, said that we too are the light of the world, carrying His light, and we need to let our light shine before men (see Matt. 5:14-16).

In these days, it is not hard to see that the world has grown darker and is in great need of Jesus; those who are Christians must let their lights shine by both living the Gospel and sharing it. When we do this, we are fulfilling the spiritual announcement that issued from God's lips, "Let there be light." He wants us to let the light of His Son Jesus shine through us. If we would take this to heart and really capture God's love and concern for people, then we would tell others about Jesus more readily and be shocked by the results!

In the story that follows, this is exactly what I was determined to do—let my light shine before others. This story may be bold for some, but I want you to see what can happen if you let God use you at any level: you will shine light into darkness and see people won to the Lord!

At this time, I hadn't been a Christian for long, perhaps a couple of years, and I wanted to tell others of my new experience with Jesus. I decided to go with a group of people and share my faith in a pizza restaurant in a city across the river. It was a Friday night after a high school game, and the place was packed with people. I began to initiate conversation with a few people at a table, just trying to establish common ground and favor with them. The conversation quickly turned to the subject of the Lord, and soon the majority of the restaurant surrounded me as I preached the Gospel. I remember feeling such a powerful presence of God as I shared my faith, letting my light shine. People were being visibly touched by the message and the power of the Holy Spirit until the manager angrily interrupted what was one of my very first public sermons.

He insisted that I stop and suggested that nobody wanted to hear what I was saying; I was to take my message outside. Well, I didn't want to be rude to the manager, so I told the people that if they wanted to continue to hear what I had to say, they could follow me outside.

Now, who in their right mind would follow this pizza preacher outside into the frigid weather? It was the dead of winter and dangerously cold outside. I started to walk out the door, and to my amazement, most of the people in that pizza place followed me! I could hardly believe it. They followed me next door to an area where there were steps leading to a large platform, which I turned into my pulpit. I was shocked as I looked down the steps at a large crowd listening to my message in the freezing cold. I was letting my light shine, and God was backing me up!

There was only one problem—and it wasn't the cold. It was that I had never led a large crowd to receive Jesus in their hearts. So, I told the people, "If you want Jesus in your heart, I want you to do something bold: get on your hands and knees and crawl to accept the Lord." I know that was bold, and it seemed crazy as it came out my mouth. You know what? They did it! They started crawling and crying—not at all concerned about the people around them. What happened next is even more amazing—because I didn't know what to do. I told them to stay put, and I went to get my friend, who was close by; he came and finished the wintery crusade, leading them in the prayer of salvation! That night it was dark both naturally and spiritually, but we let our light shine, and I am glad we did. Many people prayed a prayer of salvation that night!

My witnessing that evening was part of the fulfillment of that prophetic announcement: "Let there be light"! Our light is our testimony to a dark world; it is the truth of what Jesus came to the earth to do for us. He came to bring hope, love, forgiveness, joy, and peace; this is the light that lifts the darkness in our hearts. This is what happened in Jesus' ministry everywhere He went—He brought that light to people.

We need to "let there be light" everywhere we go, and we need to let that light shine because people are so much on God's heart. There are so many God wants to reach, but the devil has blinded their eyes, keeping them in spiritual darkness. The Bible calls him the god of this world:

> *But if our gospel be hid, it is hid to them that are lost: In whom the god of this world hath blinded the minds of them which believe not, lest the light of the glorious gospel of Christ, who is the image of God, should shine unto them* (2 Corinthians 4:3-4).

The devil doesn't want us to let our light shine. He tries to stop us by making us timid, distracted, and afraid of rejection or harm, so that we don't step out and try. But we need to try; if we don't let our light shine, then people will remain in spiritual darkness and blindness. It is our responsibility to reach people so we can bring them out of darkness into His marvelous light, no matter who they are! It is sad to think that many who need a real relationship with Jesus are not necessarily heathens in the streets selling drugs or committing murder; they are those in churches who never hear the Gospel message or aren't given an opportunity to truly commit their lives to the Lord.

But of further concern is the possibility that not only are there those who attend churches who will not go to Heaven, but also individuals who are in ministry, and even preaching behind pulpits who might not go either. For some in the ministry, their title represents a job or a deep desire to help people. While there is nothing wrong with perceiving ministry in these ways, it is dangerous when you can "do" ministry without really knowing Jesus or being able to tell others how to make it to Heaven. This has happened with some ministers and even congregations because the devil has used religion to blind and deceive their hearts. He deceives them into thinking it is their good works or some form of religious ritual or tradition that brings them to a place of salvation. Jesus said there is only one way to Heaven, and that is through Him. We must commit, believe, cling to, trust, and rely on Him in everything. It is not just a belief system; it is a daily loving, seeking, and serving of Jesus that entitles us to eternal life through Him (see Matt. 7:21-23).

To better illustrate what I mean, let me share another personal story. I remember when I was hungry to know if there was a God, before I truly became a Christian. I was asking myself questions like, "Who is this God?" and "Why am I here on planet Earth?" A further nuisance at that time was that I seemed to be getting approached by every "Jesus Freak" in the vicinity telling me I needed to be born again. I thought, *I'm already born. Can't you see that I am struggling with why I was born and why I'm here on earth? I certainly don't want to be born again! Why would I want to be born twice when I can't figure out this first birth?* I didn't realize what Jesus meant in John 3—to be born again was a reference to a spiritual rebirth because when Adam sinned, a spiritual and physical death was passed to everyone born into this world (see Rom. 3:23). Because our human blood was polluted with sin, we needed Someone pure and spotless to purchase us back and put us in right standing again with God:

> *None eye pitied thee, to do any of these unto thee, to have compassion upon thee; but thou wast cast out in the open field, to the lothing of thy person, in the day that thou wast born. And when I passed by thee, and saw thee polluted in thine own blood, I said unto thee when thou wast in thy blood, Live; yea, I said unto thee when thou wast in thy blood, Live (Ezekiel 16:5-6).*

Thank You, Jesus, for what You did for us! We may be born into this natural world with sin-polluted blood, but once we accept Jesus as our Savior and Lord, then we are born again spiritually and become spiritually alive, adopted by God as His sons and daughters!

There I was—polluted in my sinful state and lost without Jesus. I was desperate and hungry to know if God was real. So every time I was bombarded by a "Bible thumper," I began to ask questions. I thought I would ask a minister who frequented the place where I worked to get my answer. I simply asked him, "How does a person get to Heaven?" He stuttered and practically swallowed the pipe he was smoking, so I repeated my simple question. "How does a person get to Heaven? I really want to go there. I want to know." He finally got his composure and put his hand upon my shoulder and said, "That is a great question that many people want to know. Keep it up, son, and one day you will find the answer." *"No,"* I said, "I want to know now!" He said, "Well, just be good and don't break too many of the Ten Commandments."

What? I thought, *This is a minister, and he doesn't even know.* I have tried to be good, but what is "good" anyway? Besides, I don't even know all the commandments. I replied, "I am trying to be good, but I was told that we have all sinned, and there is no one righteous." I was only repeating what I had heard the so-called "Jesus Freaks" tell me. He then sighed as if he wasn't sure of himself. "Well, it sounds like you got it figured out. I am sure you will probably make it, son," he said as he departed.

Do you see my point? There are ministers and people in their churches who may never come to the knowledge of the truth because their leader doesn't have a living relationship with Jesus or know how to bring others to salvation. People are then often led to believe a lie or a false belief system based on personal standards of righteousness and good works! This is why I believe we are going to see, as we did in the days of Jesus' ministry, whole multitudes leave the city to go to the desert to be with Him! People want the real, so they are going to leave man-made traditions and religion—like the city, which is built by man. They will then seek God in a desert or a place made by God, where they can be with Him unhindered by religious traditions that never bring us to salvation or a righteous lifestyle!

This is why "Let there be light" was a prophetic announcement and proclamation that would permeate everything in creation. God was announcing His Son as the answer for all people, regardless of their situation or condition. When God uttered those first words, He was declaring a mystery that would be the answer for a dark world and a fallen man: "Let there be light!" Think of all that command refers to: a natural light; a spiritual light that would manifest both spiritually and naturally; and the Son of God Himself who would come into the world and light all men!

> *There was a man sent from God, whose name was John. The same came for a witness, to bear witness of the Light, that all men through him might believe. He was not that Light, but was sent to bear witness of that Light. That was the true Light, which lighteth every man that cometh into the world* (John 1:6-9).

The Light that this verse speaks of was not John the Baptist, but Jesus—the true Light who brings us out of darkness into the light of truth and salvation. Before creation, this wonderful Light was spoken forth to be the answer for a dark world; wise men would seek this Light; shepherds would gather themselves and their flocks to see it. This Light would bring peace on earth and goodwill toward all people. In the fullness of time, God sent Jesus, the true Light! He would come to earth as the plan of God predestined before time—a baby born in a manger who would grow to manhood, walking with His Father; who would be beaten, bruised, spit on, and crucified on a cross for all humankind.

It is now up to you and me to keep declaring, "Let there be light!" How do we do that? By letting our lights shine before all as the Lord instructed us. This is accomplished when we live a true sold-out, dedicated, committed life to Jesus, when we live honorably before the Lord and righteously before men. We let our lights shine when we boldly and unashamedly open our mouths to testify of our new life in the Lord and share the Gospel. When we do, we are in a sense saying, "Let there be Light"; "Let there be Jesus"! God has always had us on His heart, even before time!

WITHOUT FORM, VOID, AND DARK: THE CONDITION OF MAN REVEALED

I am convinced that it wasn't just natural light that was on God's heart when He spoke, "Let there be light." He was proclaiming a prophetic answer to a world that would need light to shine upon them. He spoke this not only because of the physical condition of the earth, but also because He knew that our spiritual condition would require a Savior. Let's look at this a little more closely. God spoke, "Let there be light," because the condition of the earth was without form, dark, and void:

> In the beginning God created the heaven and the earth. And the earth was without form, and void; and darkness was upon the face of the deep. And the Spirit of God moved upon the face of the waters. And God said, Let there be light: and there was light (Genesis 1:1-3).

In the same way, we have been without God, dark and void; we need the true Light, Jesus Christ. Some of us have been caught up in a religious experience; we have attended church and kept our religious traditions, or had a belief in Jesus without really knowing Him; we have needed a true salvation experience according to the Bible. We find in Scripture that there were those who had a "religious experience" with God but really didn't know Him. Some were devout in their faith and had a form of godliness, but they never came to the knowledge of the truth! *"Ever learning, and never able to come to the knowledge of the truth"* (2 Tim. 3:7).

In the Bible we see some examples of those who needed a true salvation experience. For example, there were devout Jews on the day of Pentecost who practiced religious traditions and attended temple meetings regularly. However, Peter commanded they repent and turn to Jesus as their Lord and Savior! (See Acts 2:5, 36-38.) Then we find an Ethiopian eunuch returning from Jerusalem where he had gone to worship; he was sitting in his chariot reading Scripture—yet he hadn't committed his life to Jesus to be saved! (See Acts 8:27-28, 35-38.) We also find Cornelius, a devout person who was faithful to his religious experience and gave faithfully to the poor. Yet he too still needed salvation (see Acts 10:1-6; 11:14). How about Lydia, who was a worshiper of God and regularly kept the Sabbath? Even she wasn't converted to Christianity (see Acts 16:13-14). Finally, there was Saul, who thought he was doing the Lord's will by persecuting and killing Christians, until he literally "saw the Light." (See Acts 9; Acts 26:9; Galatians 1:14.)

We find, from these examples, the same thing in the earth today and throughout history. There are many who are like the condition of the earth on the first day of creation. They are without form, void, and dark; this is exactly how we are without God, forever searching for true happiness, peace, or anything stable. We might be a church attendee, a nice person, or the worst heathen to walk the earth. Without the Light, Jesus Christ, and a real salvation experience, we will look to replace that void, that emptiness, with other things, or we will make ourselves busy to help pass the time. We might even attend church, sing in the choir, or teach Sunday school—but we have never come to the "true Light" of a committed life of loving and serving Jesus daily! We need Jesus, the Savior who can bring light to our darkness, joy to our emptiness, and stability to our empty lives.

We can't exist without natural light; it is in everything, and it has been moving from the moment God spoke it into existence. Lives that are void, without form, and dark desperately need Jesus, the true Light. This is why you and I need to tell them. We must do what the children's song says, "This little light of mine, I'm going to let it shine, let it shine, let it shine"…everywhere! Can you hear it?

God is saying, "Let My light shine through you in a dark world that needs Me!" Jesus is the answer for the world today, and you and I have been entrusted with the good news of the Gospel. People are living without hope; they often start to question God, His existence, and whether He really cares about them. Psalm 142 describes aptly the hopeless feelings of those who live with that inner emptiness: "*I looked on my right hand, and beheld, but there was no man that would know me: refuge failed me; no man cared for my soul*" (Ps. 142:4).

This reminds me of a time when I was street witnessing with a small group by Lake Michigan in Chicago, Illinois. As a group, we walked along the shore, sharing the Gospel with many as we went. Some started talking about the Lord with two college-aged women. The group wasn't having any success ministering to them as one woman in particular was very vocal and resistant. I kept feeling in my heart that the roadblocks we were encountering from her were due to the fact that she was running from God. I prayed quietly, asking the Lord what to do, and the Holy Spirit began revealing to me some things about her life.

I decided to ask her if I could share something that was on God's heart about her. She looked at me with such a look of anger and hatred. She said, "God doesn't care about me." I replied, "Yes, He does, and He wants me to tell you something about your life, so you know He really does care." The Holy Spirit had me share details about her life and what was going on. I mentioned to her that she grew up in a Christian family and had since moved out to pursue her life. I told her that she was running from God, angry at Him, and she was in an abusive relationship. She began to cry, right there on the shore of Lake Michigan. The other female team members prayed for her and ministered to her. The two women were so overcome by God and what He had revealed that they both gave their hearts to the Lord.

I will never forget what she said as we were leaving: "It was as if God stopped the whole world for me. He loved me so much to share details no one knew but God alone. He really does care for me! He showed it in such an incredible way. I'm going home to get it right with my family." Praise God for what the Lord did! She had felt empty and alone; only God knew the void, the darkness in her life. He spoke to her prophetically to show her that He is the Light for her darkness, the Peace for the void in her life, and the Rock to bring stability.

Truly, we have always been on His heart. He will stop the whole world to speak to just one!

WHAT'S ON GOD'S MIND?

I hope at this point it's not hard to guess what was really on God's mind before the foundation of the earth. We were! We are. Scripture says, *"Greater love has no one than this, than to lay down one's life for his friends"* (John 15:13 NKJV). And that is exactly what Jesus did! He is the Lord of salvation and wants everyone saved, including your whole family! "Even my family?" you might be asking. Yes, even your family—because He is also the God of household salvation! Be encouraged as you continue to read this book; we are going discover how to reach not only our families but our loved ones, friends, and those we meet. We are going to get honest with God and ourselves.

It is vitally important that we comprehend just how much people mean to the Lord and how much He wants us to reach them for Him. God loves people; He wants to reach those who feel they are in darkness and without hope. We must not forget that God made good with His promise to send His Son Jesus as the promised Messiah to save humankind. We must remember that on the night of His birth it was proclaimed, *"On earth peace, good will toward men"* (Luke 2:14). We must hold close to our hearts the commission He gave us to be fishers of men, bringing them to a personal relationship with Him. And we must always take a moment to remember and thank Jesus for the great price He paid when He died for us. All of these are but further proof and reminders that God has something very special on His heart—people.

The Bible gives countless examples of this fact. He is waiting for every last person who will turn to Him before He returns to the earth! The precious fruit of human souls is what is delaying His return:

> Be patient therefore, brethren, unto the coming of the Lord. Behold, the husbandman waiteth for the precious fruit of the earth, and hath long patience for it, until he receive the early and latter rain (James 5:7).

We need to love souls as God does. He was willing to send His only Son to suffer punishment as a lamb led to a slaughter (see Isa. 53:7). We must grasp how important we are to the Lord.

Let's look more closely at Luke 15. The whole chapter is dedicated to God's love for people and the good news that they can be saved! Jesus addressed religious folks because they were angry that He was speaking to sinners: *"And the Pharisees and scribes murmured, saying, This man receiveth sinners, and eateth with them"* (Luke 15:2). Jesus knew what was in their hearts, so He spoke to them in parables that revealed His love for lost souls. He began by telling the story of a shepherd who loses one sheep and leaves the other ninety-nine to find it: *"What man of you, having an hundred sheep, if he lose one of them, doth not leave the ninety and nine in the wilderness, and go after that which is lost, until he find it?"* (Luke 15:4). When the shepherd finds the lost sheep, *"he layeth it on his shoulders, rejoicing. And when he cometh home, he calleth together his friends and neighbours, saying*

unto them, Rejoice with me; for I have found my sheep which was lost"
(Luke 15:5-6). The shepherd's heart for the lost one, his search as
well as his celebration, reveal Jesus' love for every soul.

Jesus then described a woman who loses a coin and searches until
she finds it: *"Either what woman having ten pieces of silver, if she lose one
piece, doth not light a candle, and sweep the house, and seek diligently till
she find it?"* (Luke 15:8). Once again, He spoke of the value of one
person in the eyes of God, who continues to pursue each of us. This
needs to be our approach as well; remember, "Let there be light!" It
is up to us to let the light of our Christian lives and testimony shine
so lost souls can be found like this lost coin!

Notice again, how God regards the finding of a lost soul:

> *And when she hath found it, she calleth her friends and
> her neighbours together, saying, Rejoice with me; for I
> have found the piece which I had lost. Likewise, I say
> unto you, there is joy in the presence of the angels of God
> over one sinner that repenteth* (Luke 15:9-10).

God and His angels get joyful over one sinner who repents and
commits his life to Jesus. They love seeing someone get saved, but
they also get excited every time a believer steps out to share the
Gospel.

Jesus shared one more example with the scribes and Pharisees;
He told the all-too-famous story of the prodigal son who left his
father's house after receiving his inheritance prematurely. Once he
receives this inheritance from his father, he travels to a far country,
gets into trouble, and is left with nothing! *"...and there wasted his
substance with riotous living. And when he had spent all, there arose a
mighty famine in that land; and he began to be in want"* (Luke 15:13-14).
This lost son is now at his lowest, so hungry he wants to eat the food

given to swine. It is not until he comes to himself that he returns to his father's house, unsure of his welcome.

As this young prodigal nears his home, while *"he was yet a great way off, his father saw him, and had compassion, and ran, and fell on his neck, and kissed him"* (Luke 15:20). What an amazing love! Through the response of the father, Jesus shows God's attitude toward someone who is lost and needs God. The father has been watching and comes running for his lost son. God the Father looks at us with this same compassion; He pursued us by sending Jesus, and He continues to extend His love, longing to embrace us and welcome us home as sons and daughters.

I pray that you are getting a renewed sense of God's love for yourself and others. As you continue to read the pages of this book, let His love further stir you and increase the brightness of your light. Remember that forever decision God made before we were created, as well as His powerful prophetic announcement: "Let there be light." Jesus is that true Light, and we are to let Him shine through us on the earth. Are you ready to be part of that prophetic announcement and let your light shine? May you be empowered to do just that!

Chapter Three

ASLEEP IN THE HARVEST

He that gathereth in summer is a wise son: but he that

sleepeth in harvest is a son that causeth shame

(Proverbs 10:5).

As a young boy, I took a job working in a bean field. My job was to walk through crops of beans and cut out any weeds or corn stalks from previous years so they wouldn't choke out this year's harvest. On one of those early, hot summer days, I was dragging myself through the bean fields. It was hot, muggy, and wet; I felt like a cow in a farm field—bugs were biting and landing on me every second. I was tired and didn't want to work that day; besides, it was a long walk through those fields. I just kept lagging farther and farther behind the rest of the group until they were completely out of sight. At this time, I thought, *Great!* I decided I was going to get a little sleep under a tree and catch up with the small team later.

Well, you guessed it; I fell asleep in the midst of the bean field until I was awakened by a very angry foreman! I wanted to keep sleeping, but the foreman wouldn't let me. Even though I was just a young boy, I had a job to do, and I wasn't doing it. I thought taking a brief nap wouldn't hurt anything, but I was wrong—you can affect the outcome of the harvest when you are asleep in it!

This is exactly what Proverbs 10:5 says: *"He that gathereth in summer is a wise son: but he that sleepeth in harvest is a son that causeth shame."* I was doing what this verse states; I was sleeping in the harvest field instead of working! Now mine was a natural harvest, but what about being spiritually asleep in the spiritual harvest of people's lives?

ASLEEP IN THE HARVEST!

Sadly, many people are living this way—spiritually asleep in the harvest. They are unconcerned, lazy, and unaware of a world dying around them. In the bean field, I had a job to do to, and that was not to allow weeds to grow and choke out the harvest of beans. I was also expected to work and not be found sleeping! In terms of the spiritual harvest, if we were to ask ourselves some very sobering questions, we might be saddened by our own answers. For instance, when was the last time we talked to somebody about the Gospel or led someone to the Lord? Or, when was the last time someone gave his or her heart to the Lord and had a true biblical conversion in our churches?

I am sure some may be able to answer these questions better than others because they do try to share the Gospel regularly. However, the truth is, many of us couldn't answer these questions very positively—and neither could many churches. This is hurtful to the Lord because people are and have always been on God's heart, as we clearly saw in the previous chapter. It is our responsibility to reach them. Jesus died on the cross, rose from the dead, and left the responsibility of the harvest of souls to you and me. We are commanded by God to go into the entire world and preach the Gospel. It is our responsibility, and we must receive the Lord's burden for such a task. It is up to us; we have to wake up and reach them!

I am convinced that this "asleep in the harvest" mentality holds back many God-loving people and churches. If we are not careful, we can slip into spiritual apathy and busyness; we can assume the burden of responsibility is upon someone else and never reach the people around us who are dying every second without Jesus. *We must shake off this sleep!* So often we allow this asleep in the harvest mentality to render us ineffective in the battle to win souls. The burden of God for lost humanity must be in our hearts to reach a world that desperately needs Him.

It has become common for believers to enjoy their lives and the churches they attend with all the programs offered, but take very little effort to win people to Jesus. Such believers are like the children of Israel in the book of Judges when they were confined in their caves (what we might call the four walls of the church) afraid of the enemy:

Yet again the People of Israel went back to doing evil in God's sight. God put them under the domination of Midian for seven years. Midian overpowered Israel. Because of Midian, the People of Israel made for themselves hideouts in the mountains—caves and forts... (Judges 6:1-6 MSG).

Israel was living in such fear of the enemy that it eventually affected their ability to gather the harvest. The enemy intimidated them, causing them to live within the four walls of their hideouts, and destroyed their harvest:

When Israel planted its crops, Midian and Amalek, the easterners, would invade them, camp in their fields, and destroy their crops all the way down to Gaza. They left nothing for them to live on... (Judges 6:1-6 MSG).

In the same way, many of us have allowed the enemy to bring us into bondage to our own fear, complacency, and apathy so that we have established our own strongholds. These strongholds can be the four walls of our churches that confine us from reaching out to a world that needs Jesus. Or perhaps we build up walls of fear, laziness, and other excuses so that we never tell anyone about the Lord or try to share the Gospel—as a result, the harvest is being destroyed.

I have found that there are generally three common excuses when it comes both to sharing our faith and responding to God's invitation of eternal life in Heaven. We find these excuses in Luke 14 when Jesus tells a story of a certain man who had a desire to host a great feast and sent his servant out with invitations. We know from this story that Jesus is speaking metaphorically: the great feast is the marriage supper of the Lamb that will be served in Heaven at the end of all things, and the servant is Jesus—but we have the same responsibility to invite people by sharing the Gospel of Jesus Christ with them. As Jesus tells the story, we see that the servant is met with excuses from those invited to the dinner: *"And they all with one consent began to make excuse"* (Luke 14:18). These excuses fall into three categories:

- The excuse of the distraction of possessions, interests, investments, and hobbies: *"I have bought a piece of ground, and I must needs go and see it: I pray thee have me excused"* (Luke 14:18).

- The excuse of the demands of work (businesses, jobs, responsibilities): *"And another said, I have bought five yoke of oxen, and I go to prove them: I pray thee have me excused"* (Luke 14:19).

- The excuse of family relationships and commitments: *"...and another said, I have married a wife, and therefore I cannot come"* (Luke 14:20).

When the master of the feast (our heavenly Father) heard of these excuses, he became very angry. These individuals loved their businesses, jobs, lives, families, and possessions more than God and the souls of men and women! These excuses caused them to miss out on Heaven's invitation because they were willing to invest greatly in their temporal possessions but meanly in eternal things. The excuses they used are the same ones that cause us to be asleep in the harvest. They were so naturally preoccupied that they were spiritually asleep.

What is even more sobering for us is God's response to those who adopted these excuses; the master of the feast in this parable was *angry* that they made excuses and refused the invitation! Let's look at His response and the instruction that was given:

The servant returned and told his master what they had said. His master was furious and said, "Go quickly into the streets and alleys of the town and invite the poor, the crippled, the blind, and the lame" (Luke 14:21 NLT).

This parable makes it very clear that we must make Heaven and the invitation of salvation a priority. We must go out into the "streets and alleys" compelling people to come to Him. The world is not getting any better, but growing darker: *"Sin will be rampant everywhere, and the love of many will grow cold"* (Matt. 24:12 NLT).

In Second Timothy, we find the apostle Paul mentioning just how dangerous and sinful some people will get in the "perilous" last days. People will be boastful, lovers of pleasure more than lovers of God, unthankful, unholy, disobedient to parents, trucebreakers, and fierce, to name a few (see 2 Tim. 3:1-7). These descriptions highlight why it is crucial that we wake up and become alert to the people dying around us without the Lord. The only real answer for humanity is Jesus, and the only one who can rescue us from our wicked condition is the Lord. We must take the Gospel seriously and share it with as many as we meet.

Sometimes people don't want to share their faith because they are at ease in their walk with God (see Amos 6:1). They have become comfortable with their hobbies, money, homes, occupations, and their 2.5 kids. They love attending a church and staying in its four walls, which requires little if any commitment to reach the lost. Yet, Jesus wants His people to wake up from a spiritual "asleep in the harvest" mentality and begin to reach people for Him. This is what the Lord says about the fields of harvest:

Say not ye, There are yet four months, and then cometh harvest? behold, I say unto you, Lift up your eyes, and look on the fields; for they are white already to harvest (John 4:35).

We can learn a lot from this verse about being alert in the spiritual harvest. Jesus shows us the process:

- *Say not, there are four months, then harvest:* We are not to have the attitude that reaching people can wait for another time or that it isn't urgent.

- *Lift up your eyes:* We are to become focused on winning souls because it is our responsibility. It is time for us to wake up and look after lost humanity rather than just our own needs!

- *Look on the fields:* We should start looking for ways to use our lives, time, money, resources, and talents to reach people.

- *They are white already for harvest:* We must be willing to share the Gospel because people are ready, waiting for someone to reach them!

Why did Jesus refer to the harvest as being "white already to harvest"? Because that is the point of critical mass. If we don't gather the harvest when it's white and ripe, then it will fall to the ground unharvested. At this point, if it is not gathered, it is lost forever! This is why we must resist the "asleep in the harvest" mentality and be willing to lay our lives down to make a difference in the lives of others. We must shake off spiritual slumber and apathy toward the harvest. Proverbs 10:5 says it causes shame when we are asleep in the harvest: *"but he that sleepeth in harvest is a son that causeth shame."* While we are sleepy, unconcerned people, there are lives falling apart around us. Unfortunately, the urgency of the harvest doesn't even affect some Christians! We must become alert, stirred, committed, and passionate about reaching people for Him. I believe the Lord is asking us the same question He asked His disciples, who seemed to have a habit of sleeping, *"Why do you sleep?"* (see Luke 22:46).

We must open our eyes, look around us, and share the wonderful message of salvation. If we don't, we will lose a harvest of precious souls. There are many who still need to receive that invitation to live forever in Heaven, and it is now more urgent than ever to gather them in.

GATHERING THE HARVEST

We are told by the Lord that we must pray and ask Him to send people to reach lost humanity: *"The harvest truly is plentiful, but the laborers are few. Therefore pray the Lord of the harvest to send out laborers into His harvest"* (Matt. 9:37-38 NKJV). In this verse, Jesus mentioned that the spiritual harvest is greater than the few who make themselves available to labor for it. In other words, the number of people to reach with the Gospel is far greater than the few Christians who are willing to reach them. Did you notice that this verse describes the harvest as the Lord's? Simply put, the harvest is lost souls who need salvation. This means every person born into this world is someone who needs to be reached for Jesus.

Jesus used the example of a harvest field, which many believe was a wheat field, because it has many grains and turns white at harvest time. This wheat harvest also represents many people, every person in the world. If we are to labor in this harvest, there are some things we will have to do, much like reaping a natural harvest. We will have to plow, plant the seed, water, and then gather the harvest.

- *Plow and till the soil* (see Rom. 10:13-14). This comes by prayer, planning, and interceding for hearts to be open to the Gospel before we share it. When we prepare in this way, hardened hearts can become soft and open to the Gospel. We are also obeying Jesus' command: praying for the Lord to send laborers to reach His harvest!

- *Share the Gospel by sowing a seed.* Some plant a seed by sharing the Gospel, and others water through prayer (see 1 Cor. 3:7-8). Yet, it is God who gives the increase. You cannot have a harvest unless someone plants a seed by sharing the good news of eternal life through Jesus.

- *You have to water the seed* (see Ps. 126:5-6). We do this through prayer and crying out to God for lost souls. When we pray for those we are trying to reach, our prayers of compassion and burden can cause people's hearts to grow closer to the Lord. We also water the seed by doing kind acts of love, which only enhance the seeds of the Gospel that we have planted.

- *We then are to gather the harvest* (see John 4:36-38). We do this by sharing our faith, inviting people to church, praying, leading them in a prayer of salvation, and discipling new believers.

As we can see, we are the laborers God is counting on; we must work at plowing, planting, watering, and gathering people to live forever in Heaven. God wants everyone to come to His grand dinner and make Heaven their eternal home: "*And the lord said unto the servant, Go out into the highways and hedges, and compel them to come in, that my house may be filled*" (Luke 14:23). This verse helps us to see that God wants His house full. He wants you, me, our families, our loved ones, friends, acquaintances, and everyone we meet to be with Him forever!

But a full house requires people who are willing to work in His harvest by ministering the Gospel to others! This is what Jesus trained His disciples to do; He commissioned them to go into all the world, preaching the Gospel to everyone. We have been given the same job description. We are to evangelize and preach this Gospel to as many people as possible. If we don't, then how will people hear the message of salvation?

> ...And how can they believe in him if they have never heard about him? And how can they hear about him unless someone tells them? (Romans 10:14 NLT)

We are the ones who are supposed to tell them. We are those laborers that Jesus is looking for! Reaching the harvest is every Christian's duty—yours and mine.

In order to fulfill the commission, we must have the same heart and prayer that Isaiah did: "Lord, here am I. Send me." For some of us, that prayer sounds more like, "Here I am, Lord, send others!" We have to put our excuses aside because we have all been called by God to be ministers of reconciliation. As Christians, we have the sole responsibility to share the message of salvation that reconciles, or brings people back, to their loving God through Jesus. After reading this, you might be saying, "Yeah, but evangelism just isn't my thing—and to top it off, I'm not even a preacher!"

I had people tell me that when I used to conduct evangelism outreaches at the church I attended when I first got saved. I had started off just trying to share my faith with friends, co-workers, and people I would meet in public, but it soon became something that I did faithfully, leading teams to minister at various places around my city. Once I had a true understanding of my responsibility to reach the lost and had the joy of seeing someone's life touched, the results were incredible!

When I first started the outreaches, I would invite other Christians to come out and share their faith. I was surprised at how many would say it wasn't their thing. We would see whole crowds come to the Lord on any given weekend, often picking the new converts up with the church van or buses to attend one of the services. Eventually, what started with just a few people blossomed into a real evangelism focus for the whole church. People couldn't deny the church growth or the renewed fire when people put aside their schedules, agendas, and excuses and began to realize they were called to evangelize. People who never thought God could use them had awesome testimonies of salvations and lives getting touched by God! I want to exhort you not to disqualify yourself or feel that you can't do it.

It is easy to disqualify ourselves for many reasons, but let's look at the definition of *evangelism* and what it means to preach or evangelize. When we look at the Scriptures, we find that the actual word *evangelism* is not found in the Bible. Yet, the concept is in Scripture, and some translations may use the word. However, we do find two similar words: *evangelist* and *evangelize*.

The word evangelize comes from a Greek noun, *euaggelion*, which means glad tidings or good news.[1] *"And this **gospel** of the kingdom shall be preached in all the world for a witness unto all nations; and then shall the end come"* (Matt. 24:14).

The word evangelist in the Greek is *euaggelistés*, which means an evangelist, a missionary, bearer of good tidings.[2] *"...and we entered into the house of Philip the **evangelist**, which was one of the seven; and abode with him"* (Acts 21:8).

Now, there is also the Greek verb *euaggelizó*, which means to announce good news or to preach the Gospel.[3] This describes what we commonly refer to as evangelism because it is an action of telling the message of the Gospel: *"And the angel said unto them, Fear not: for, behold, I bring you **good tidings** of great joy, which shall be to all people"* (Luke 2:10). In summary, the word *evangelism* simply means to make known the Gospel message.

As we look at the word preach, we find that it is sometimes translated from the Greek verb *kerusso*, which means to be a herald, to proclaim; to *preach* (announce) a message publicly and with conviction (persuasion).[4] This is important to know because when we are proclaiming Jesus, we are preaching, or evangelizing: *"And He said unto them, 'Go ye into all the world, and **preach** the gospel to every creature'"* (Mark 16:15).

We can see from these definitions that it certainly includes every one of us who have received Jesus as our Savior and Lord. It is not just one person or one church's responsibility to reach the lost, but all of us as the Body of Christ everywhere! We are all called to preach, evangelize, and share the good news of Jesus. Sadly, this is not the conviction or burden of some Christians.

It is sobering when you think of how much more diligent and committed other religions are to spreading their message than some Christians are. This was very evident to me when a couple of men came to my door and tried to convert me to their religion. I will never forget it because they had more passion, fire, and boldness than many Christians! I tell you, when they spoke to me, I was determined to be bold back. I wasn't rude, but I was determined to let God be glorified. I felt like the prophet Elijah in his showdown with the prophets of Baal: "Let the true God answer by fire" (see 1 Kings 18:24). I invited them into my house, and they began to tell me about their beliefs. I listened for a little bit, amazed at how far off their doctrine was from Scripture. Then I kindly interrupted and said, "Let's pray. You pray to your god, and I will pray to mine." I asked them to go first. Yet, after stuttering and getting flustered, they asked me to start. So I did! I prayed boldly to my heavenly Father in Jesus' name.

Then I began to pray strong in the spirit, and I mean strong. I stopped only to hear them clicking their briefcases closed and looking like they had seen a ghost. They probably did...I mean the Holy Ghost! They left in a sweat and in a hurry! However, the story doesn't end there. I began to follow them to the next couple of houses. I told them I was going to every house with them because my neighborhood belonged to Jesus, and I wasn't going to settle for anything less. They got the hint after a couple of homes and sped away in their car!

You have to give them credit; at least they were bold and passionate about what they believed, more so than many Christians. This needs to be our approach to the Gospel with which we have been entrusted. We must be willing to share it in a bold, polite, and powerful way. We need people who will take a bold and unashamed stand for Jesus, as I did that day. I wasn't rude or unmannerly; I was passionate and bold about the truth!

BOLDNESS FOR THE HARVEST

You might still be thinking, *But, Hank, I'm just not a bold person; it isn't my personality.* I can certainly understand how you feel, except boldness isn't necessarily a personality. I have found that boldness is not based on your personality or whether you are outgoing or shy; rather, it is a mindset and attitude given by the Lord if we will ask Him. If we are going to reach people for the Lord and gather the harvest of souls, we must have boldness. This is what the early church did when they were being persecuted for their faith. They prayed for more boldness: *"And now, Lord, behold their threatenings: and grant unto thy servants, that with all boldness they may speak thy word"* (Acts 4:29).

You can actually obtain a life of greater spiritual boldness by praying for it and then stepping out in it. The most shy, reserved person can be powerfully used of God in boldness because he or she recognizes that it is a spiritual endowment given by the Lord. We should not approach spiritual boldness with the mindset that it may work for others, but not for me. Spiritual boldness is pretty simple to understand because it involves making a courageous decision to speak the Gospel with openness, confidence, and freedom.

The apostle Paul could be bold and not ashamed of the Gospel because he recognized that there is power given to share and to demonstrate God's wonders as a sign to the unbeliever: *"For I am not ashamed of the gospel of Christ: for it is the power of God unto salvation to every one that believeth; to the Jew first, and also to the Greek"* (Rom. 1:16). This needs to be our approach and prayer as well—we are unashamed to share our faith. If we lack boldness, then we need to continue to pray for it and take steps to share the Gospel.

The early church was bold, passionate, wild, and just plain determined to reach the lost. In the midst of being persecuted, they prayed for more boldness. Now, this didn't mean they were rude, obnoxious, or flakey. We don't want to confuse rudeness with boldness. What we want to do is allow God to stretch us in who we are and in our efforts to reach the lost. This comes by understanding what Holy Spirit boldness looks like—as we see it, for example, in the early days of the churches in Acts. The Holy Spirit and His power caused growth, a ruckus, and powerful manifestations. It seems the bolder believers were, the more power was manifested, and the more the church grew.

This kind of boldness and spiritual power is rarely found in many of today's churches that profess Christianity. Human traditions and religious mindsets have hindered many in the Body of Christ from being bold about the Gospel, so they don't remotely look or act like the church we see in the book of Acts. Some churches have become mere social clubs, seeker friendly, and void of God's power. Some churches rarely emphasize the importance of reaching the lost! They exhibit very little spiritual boldness or an awareness of the need to reach lost souls.

This was not the case of the church in Acts, or their leaders. They were bold and unashamed for the Gospel, literally putting their lives on the line to preach it.

Think of the amazing spiritual transformation of the apostle Peter who denied Jesus three times and was then overtaken with boldness by the Holy Spirit's power because of the Spirit's outpouring in Acts 2. He now stands up boldly to speak. However, it wasn't a feeling or his personality, but rather the Holy Spirit giving him the boldness and the words to speak: *"But Peter, standing up with the eleven, lifted up his voice, and said unto them..."* (Acts 2:14).

Notice how the Holy Spirit's infilling added to his boldness and message:

- *"For these are not drunken, **as ye suppose"*** (Acts 2:15). Peter confronted and corrected them!

- *"Jesus of Nazareth, a man approved of God among you by miracles and wonders and signs, which God did by Him in the midst of you, **as ye yourselves also know"*** (Acts 2:22). He reminded them that they knew the truth.

- *"...ye have taken, and **by wicked hands have crucified and slain"*** (Acts 2:23). He held them responsible for crucifying the Lord!

- *"...that God hath made the same Jesus, **whom ye have crucified,** both Lord and Christ"* (Acts 2:36). He testified once again to their accountability—and to the identity of the One who died.

- *"**Repent,** and be baptized every one of you..."* (Acts 2:38). He called them to repentance!

This fresh infilling of the Spirit caused Peter to receive such boldness that the religious leaders confronted him because he was preaching, casting out devils, and healing the sick boldly. His bold obedience stirred up religious demons and religious leaders to persecute and try to stop it (see Acts 4:6-7). This is usually the case when we decide to step out and share our faith. There is always someone, whether a relative or a religious spirit, who will try to stop us. This can cause us to become intimidated so that we back off and rarely, if ever, share the Gospel. For some, intimidation eventually leads to spiritual slumber regarding the harvest. The devil knows this, so he uses whatever he can, especially religious spirits, to stop your boldness! It was the religious spirits in the scribes and Pharisees that crucified Jesus and would never bow to Him because they were prideful, mean, and hated the Gospel.

These leaders were trying to stop the boldness of Peter and John when they asked them by what power they were healing the sick and ministering the Gospel (see Acts 4:7). This opposition didn't deter the apostles because they knew that boldness was necessary if the Gospel was to be preached and demonstrated. This caused the devil to be afraid of Peter and John. Don't think for a minute that he is not afraid of you also. He is most certainly afraid of you and the message you have to share, so he will try to keep you from sharing the Gospel by attacking your boldness. He hates when we are bold for the things of God because that boldness may win someone to the Lord.

When Caiaphas the High Priest saw the boldness of Peter and John, he began to be used by the devil and accused them of being ignorant and unlearned:

Now when they saw the boldness of Peter and John, and perceived that they were unlearned and ignorant men, they marvelled; and they took knowledge of them, that they had been with Jesus (Acts 4:13).

Caiaphas and the religious leaders' plan didn't work against Peter and John because their display of boldness wasn't based on personality, ignorance, or their IQ. The religious leaders couldn't figure out how the two apostles could be bold when, in their opinion, Peter and John were ignorant. Because they had been with Jesus, they manifested boldness! Did you notice something powerful about boldness in this verse? It can be seen and recognized! These religious leaders *saw* the boldness of Peter and John. They *saw* their unwavering faith and determination to preach the Gospel, ministering God's power. This boldness came from their experience in the Upper Room, staying in God's presence and receiving supernatural strength; it came from time with Jesus and the power of the Holy Spirit! Remember, you can pray for boldness and expect to see the results, just as these leaders did when they falsely accused Peter and John.

We can learn a lot about sharing the Gospel by looking at Jesus. As we look at Jesus, we see how tender and full of kindness and love He was as He ministered to sinners. When He dealt with the pride and resistance of religious people and their traditions, we find that He spoke boldly and ministered in power. Though the religious tried to hinder the Lord, this never kept Him from preaching the truth and demonstrating God's power. He kept on boldly demonstrating and proclaiming the Gospel. It didn't matter to Jesus if He experienced resistance from those to whom He was speaking; He wouldn't let their fear, anger, or intimidation stop Him. We must get free of fear and intimidation as well. We *will* face opposition—that is par for the course—but we are not to let that stop us.

Let's look at a time when Jesus was faced with those who didn't like His boldness or His message. He didn't let them stop Him from preaching the Gospel. In Luke 4, we read that He returned from the wilderness in the power of the Spirit, came to the temple, and began to read a prophetic passage from the book of Isaiah:

> And there was delivered unto him the book of the prophet Esaias. And when he had opened the book, he found the place where it was written, The Spirit of the Lord is upon me, because He hath anointed me to preach the gospel to the poor; He hath sent me to heal the brokenhearted, to preach deliverance to the captives, and recovering of sight to the blind, to set at liberty them that are bruised, to preach the acceptable year of the Lord (Luke 4:17-19).

Jesus read this Scripture announcing who He was and what He had come to do, and as He spoke further, He was met with resistance from the religious leaders. They were overcome with anger and tried to kill Him:

> And all they in the synagogue, when they heard these things, were filled with wrath, And rose up, and thrust him out of the city, and led him unto the brow of the hill whereon their city was built, that they might cast him down headlong" (Luke 4:28-29).

Praise God, they couldn't kill Him! Jesus said no man could take His life, but He laid it down of Himself (see John 10:18). It wasn't the time for Him to lay down His life, and He passed right through the murderous crowd! Likewise, the enemy will rise up with anger and intimidation to try to shut us down. Religious spirits will size us up, bring resistance and fear, and try to lull us into spiritual slumber. They tried this with Jesus, and they will try it with us as well.

There are different ways that religious spirits will try to attack your boldness:

1. Body language: *"And the eyes of all them that were in the synagogue were fastened on Him"* (Luke 4:20).

2. Words to question and size you up: *"And they said, Is not this Joseph's son?"* (Luke 4:22).

3. Anger: *"...all they in the synagogue, when they heard these things, were filled with wrath"* (Luke 4:28).

4. Threats and violent responses: *"And rose up, and thrust Him out of the city..."* (Luke 4:29).

We can't let the enemy's ploys stop us because now, more than ever, is the time to be bold about the things of God, especially with regard to lost souls. If we were to take an honest assessment today of many churches and Christians, we would see that boldness is a much-needed ingredient. It is missing from pulpits, prayer meetings, and outreach. This lack of boldness is also evident by the low numbers of churches growing by true Holy Spirit power and anointed evangelism. A lack of boldness is further seen in some Christians who seldom invite anyone to church, share their faith, or pray for someone to be saved. We must remember to be bold because the righteous are bold as lions! *"The wicked flee when no man pursueth: but the righteous are bold as a lion"* (Prov. 28:1).

Have you ever seen a bunch of chickens all clucking together? They just carry on in everyday life until the slightest noise or obstacle comes in their path. Then they begin to scurry in panic, making noise, and flapping their wings! This is how some approach sharing their faith. The slightest resistance from someone or the mere thought of reaching a lost soul sends them into "chicken panic." This is not who we are! We are to be bold as lions! Lions aren't intimidated or afraid of much; rather, they open their mouths with a roar of authority!

Begin asking the Lord for more boldness. Continue like Peter and those in the Upper Room; stay in the Lord's presence and receive a fresh infilling of the Holy Spirit's power. You will find that you are not limited by your personality or your past or your challenges. You won't be a spiritual chicken asleep in the harvest, but a bold lion winning souls to Jesus!

This is what I decided to do; I was determined to increase my boldness in sharing the Gospel. I wanted to shed my chicken feathers for a lion's mane! To do this, I thought I would approach a group of people at a local fast-food restaurant parking lot one Friday night to talk with them about the Lord. They seemed to be high school or college age. Now I realize this might be too bold for some, but it was what I felt was the necessary next step for me. I approached the group, trying to be kind and establish some common ground rather than launching out with something like, "Turn or burn!" (In all seriousness, I had small discussions with them about their cars before I began to talk about Jesus.)

As soon as I starting sharing the message of salvation, one person got straight in my face with glaring eyes and a very angry expression. He began to tell me he was the devil and described what he was going to do to me. I must admit this took me back a little because it obviously was not the response I was looking for. I guess I wasn't in the mood to meet the devil! So, I just continued to tell this person, who was impersonating Satan, about Jesus even though he got angrier. The more I spoke, the more power he lost because others in his group pulled him back and insisted that I continue! I could hardly believe it. Yet, it was my bold step that led to many of that group getting saved that night!

I understand that, for some, my example may be too bold, and I agree this may not be the next step for many. I simply want to encourage you to take those necessary steps of boldness and not fall asleep in the harvest. The key is to pray for boldness and expect God to use you. If you stay at zero, you will see zero results. If we are afraid to stretch ourselves, we may never tap into greater levels of results in seeing lost souls come to Jesus. So I encourage you to take small steps to increase your boldness. Maybe it is wearing a Christian shirt or inviting someone to church. Perhaps it is taking a bold step and sharing your faith with a co-worker or acquaintance.

You can increase your boldness just by being excited about your faith, your church, the Christian book you're reading, or something that is Christ centered. Your excitement stirs up curiosity in others. Just don't argue or be rude, and always treat people with love and respect. Always be excited about your Christianity, and do your best to represent the Lord well. Try to avoid always having a discouraged countenance when you are around the unsaved. This doesn't imply that you won't, or can't, have a bad day or go through challenges, but people need to see your joy and victory in serving the Lord. And remember, as you step out, don't let fear, lack of boldness, or rejection stop you.

As we take steps to increase our boldness, we should consider a few more things. Let's look again at what the apostles did: they prayed for boldness and spoke boldly. Pretty simple: we too can ask for boldness and then look for opportunities to speak it out. Here are some keys that we can apply to our lives:

1. Spend time in the Lord's presence and study the life of Jesus: "*...they had been with Jesus*" (Acts 4:13).

2. Ask for boldness: "*...and grant unto Thy servants, that with all boldness they may speak thy word*" (Acts 4:29).

3. Spend time in prayer, especially in the Spirit: *"And when they had prayed, the place was shaken where they were assembled together; and they were all filled with the Holy Ghost..."* (Acts 4:31).

4. Open your mouth and speak boldly: *"...they spake the word of God with boldness"* (Acts 4:31).

5. Expect boldness and use your boldness: *"And with great power gave the apostles witness of the resurrection of the Lord Jesus..."* (Acts 4:33).

We see another example of how to progress in spiritual boldness in Paul's letter to the Church of Ephesus. He maintained a life of prayer that led to boldness when he opened his mouth to speak and minister the Gospel:

> *Praying always with all prayer and supplication in the Spirit, and watching thereunto with all perseverance and supplication for all saints; And for me, that utterance may be given unto me, that I may open my mouth boldly, to make known the mystery of the gospel* (Ephesians 6:18-19).

Paul points out that those little steps, those little decisions, need to be made first in prayer and then followed up by our actions. We have to be willing to take those bold steps because it is time to gather the harvest.

As we bring this chapter to a close, let's not forget that we may receive varying reactions from people; some may receive and some may not. We need to faithfully labor and take those steps of boldness to share our faith—the increase is the Lord's.

Whatever the reaction, I want you to stay strong and realize you are equipped with God's Spirit. Furthermore, you have the testimony of what God has done in your life. Decide today to look around for those who may need the Lord. Start small and build day by day until witnessing and being a witness for the Lord becomes natural—or should I say, *supernatural!*

PRAYER FOR THE HARVEST AND BOLDNESS

Now that we are being stirred for souls, let's take a moment to ask the Lord to give us His burden for people. Let's ask Him to help us boldly proclaim His Word so we won't be found asleep in the harvest.

> Heavenly Father, I ask that You would give me a real heart and burden for people. Let me see them the way You see them. Give me a love for people as You love them, and grant me more boldness to use my life to reach others. Lord, I thank You for this, and as I reach out to others, I fully expect You to reach my family that they may be saved. Amen.

I believe God is working at this very moment in your life and in the lives of your loved ones. Continue praying to the Lord; ask Him to use you in people's lives and increase your spiritual boldness. Start expecting to see God giving you greater boldness to reach out to someone. It just takes bold steps of faith.

I know you can do it! God is counting on you!

ENDNOTES

1. *Euaggelion;* see http://concordances.org/greek/2098.htm.
2. *Euaggelistés;* see http://concordances.org/greek/2099.htm.

3. *Euaggelizó*; see http://concordances.org/greek/2097.htm.

4. *Kerusso*; see http://concordances.org/greek/2784.htm.

Chapter Four

ALL IN THE FAMILY

Tell the whole community of Israel that on the tenth day

of this month each man is to take a lamb for his family,

one for each household (Exodus 12:3 NIV).

"Help me, I'm burning; I'm burning! I'm going to die soon, and I'm scared!" he screamed. He was kicking his legs as he continued to scream, "They're going to get me; I'm burning!" These were some of the final words spoken by the grandfather of one of my church members before his death. She had gone to visit him after he suffered a serious decline in his health, and she was told by the medical staff that he would pass away within the next few days. Unprepared for news like that, she was determined to reach him before he died, concerned that he wouldn't make it to Heaven. She arrived where her grandfather was staying, and she could hear him screaming. The entire place was in turmoil.

As she entered the room, she saw extreme fear upon her grandfather's face; he kept grabbing at her, screaming for her to help him. Thank God, this woman knew how to get hold of God for her family! She sat down next to her grandfather and began to pray over him, asking for God's intervention in this crisis moment. She said she had never seen such a look of fear before on someone's face. It was evident her grandpa was dying and getting a glimpse of hell which was waiting for his lost soul.

She continued to pray and speak to him, as her grandfather told her of his fear of dying. She told him not to be scared because he would be going to Heaven. He looked at her and said, "No, no...I don't know God. I'm burning." She reassured him that he could still go to Heaven if he received Jesus as his Lord and Savior. When she asked him if he wanted to pray with her, he said yes. But the moment she began to pray, he started moving around, getting very violent and yelling at her. A spiritual battle was raging for this man's soul, so she prayed even harder. In her spirit, she was determined that she would not lose her grandfather to hell. As she prayed harder, he calmed down instantly, receiving Jesus as his Lord that day! He prayed with full understanding of what he was doing. Afterward, he took a deep breath and fell back in the bed. He was so peaceful she actually thought he had passed away, but he had just fallen asleep. Even the nurse said she noticed how peaceful the atmosphere in the room had become. This man, tormented a few hours before, was now resting through the night, a saved man.

In fact, the next day he was very happy, laughing and smiling with the family after his conversion. The woman asked her grandfather if he remembered what had happened, and he said, smiling, "Yes, I met Jesus." She and her family sat with him for a while until he fell asleep again. Her grandfather never woke up from that sleep, passing away six days later, only to awake in Heaven!

Thank God this woman knew how to pray for her family member and wouldn't give up. God wanted this man saved; all he needed was someone to take a determined, prayerful stand for his salvation. God doesn't just save individuals; He wants to save whole households. He just needs someone to cry out on earth for them to be saved as this woman did for her grandfather. Now is the time while we are alive on this earth to believe God and pray for our families to be saved. We must cry out for our families and loved ones as the rich man cried out from hell for his family to be saved as we read in Chapter One. Remember his desperate prayer to Father Abraham:

> *Then he said, I pray thee therefore, father, that thou wouldest send him* [Lazarus] *to my father's house: For I have five brethren; that he may testify unto them, lest they also come into this place of torment* (Luke 16:27-28).

The only problem was the rich man couldn't be saved himself, nor could he save his family because he was in hell. Someone on earth must get in agreement with God's promise to save families, just as this woman in my church did.

You can be that very one to reach your family. It is the Lord's desire for entire households and families to come to the saving knowledge of our Lord. If we will pray like this woman did for her grandfather and take a stand for our families, we will be amazed at what will happen. We must let this revelation that God desires to save our families sink deep within our hearts. Then nothing will be impossible, not even the hardest relative! I know some of you probably swallowed hard and gasped for air at that statement. Yes, it is true—even that mean, hard-hearted, insensitive, rude, obnoxious, heathen of a relative. No matter who they are or what they have done, not one of them is out of reach of a true salvation experience through Jesus!

A LAMB FOR YOUR HOUSE

God wants you to start expecting your family and loved ones to be saved. All through Scripture we see that the Lord values the family and wants every household to come to know Him. Family was God's idea. He created the first family unit with Adam and Eve, and years later, He instructed Noah to build an ark so that he might save his family: *"By faith Noah, being warned of God of things not seen as yet, moved with fear, prepared an ark **to the saving of his house"*** (Heb. 11:7). God has blessed families throughout history; it is His great desire that every family member be saved. He wants each person who comes to Him to make a priority of reaching their families so they can be saved as well.

We see the pattern throughout Scripture of the value God places on the family. One such example is found in the account of the first Passover where the Jewish nation was saved and protected by the blood of a lamb sacrificed for each household. It was God's idea to provide a lamb and to save family members from the snares of death: *"...each man is to take a lamb for his family, one for each household"*

(Exod. 12:3 NIV). They were to take a lamb, and if *"the household be too little for the lamb, let him and his neighbour next unto his house take it according to the number of the souls"* (Exod. 12:4). In the same way, salvation isn't just for us or for our own family; it is to be shared with others, including our neighbors. Amazing! Just as a lamb became the means of salvation for each Israelite household, Jesus the Lamb of God became the once-and-for-all means of salvation for every household—for your household and for your neighbors' household.

The lambs sacrificed for households during that first Passover were a prophetic foreshadowing of Jesus dying as the Lamb of God for every person and every household: *"Behold the Lamb of God, which taketh away the sin of the world"* (John 1:29). The Passover lamb saved not just individuals (the firstborn of both man and beast) but the entire household or family! (See Exodus 12:12-13.) The sacrificed lamb was eaten by each person, but the whole house partook of it. When the blood of the same lamb was applied to the door posts, it protected the entire family. Correspondingly, Jesus' blood was shed not just for us, as individual believers, but for our entire families— our households! In fact, notice three key references to the lamb from Exodus 12 that point to Jesus the Messiah:

- *"In the tenth day of this month they shall take to them every man **a lamb**, according to the house of their fathers, **a lamb** for an house"* (Exod. 12:3). This verse is a prophetic foreshadowing of Jesus coming to the earth in human flesh, the spotless, unblemished Lamb of God given for all the sins of humankind.

- *"And if the household be too little for **the lamb,** let him and his neighbour next unto his house take it according to the number of the souls"* (Exod. 12:4). This verse speaks prophetically of Jesus not just as a lamb, meaning someone who would give his life for another, but as *the Lamb*, meaning the *one* and *only* answer. He is the only true Messiah, the only true way to salvation, and the sole entrance into Heaven. When we accept Him as the only Lamb, we receive the benefits He provided through His death and resurrection. He is the Lamb, God Himself, the one true God.

- *"Your lamb shall be without blemish, a male of the first year"* (Exod. 12:5). This verse prophetically refers to the personal nature of Jesus as the Lamb of God. He is *your* Lamb; salvation is based upon your personal relationship with Him.

We can understand from these references of the lamb from the first Passover meal that it pointed prophetically to Jesus and salvation through Him. He is the Lamb given for the whole world and for our families. Yet, He is also our own individual, personal Lamb and God; we can become intimate in our understanding of Him.

Once, while praying, I had a life-changing vision of Jesus as the Lamb of God. In the first part of the vision, I saw a very bloody, frail, beaten lamb with its wool pulled out, dying, barely breathing. This lamb had been beaten, whipped, stripped, kicked, and left for dead. Blood was everywhere as this little lamb lay lifeless and innocent. I knew this vision was a picture of what Jesus went through for us in His crucifixion:

> *...and the LORD hath laid on Him the iniquity of us all. He was oppressed, and he was afflicted, yet he opened not his mouth: He is brought as a lamb to the slaughter, and as a sheep before her shearers is dumb, so he openeth not his mouth* (Isaiah 53:6-7).

As the vision continued, I now saw this same lamb being transformed before my eyes; He stood, with beautiful white wool and a golden crown upon His head, before a huge throne. This lamb looked new, powerful, and the only evidence of what He had once suffered was His scars. I knew I was seeing the resurrected Jesus worshiped by all Heaven as the Lamb of God who was worthy to be slain: *"Worthy is the Lamb that was slain to receive power, and riches, and wisdom, and strength, and honour, and glory, and blessing"* (Rev. 5:12).

Then, in my vision, the Lord said that every person must have this double revelation of the Lamb: crucified and bloodied as the Savior for the whole world; and gloriously resurrected as Lord of all! Revelation references both of these pictures of the Lamb:

> *And I beheld, and, lo, in the midst of the throne and of the four beasts, and in the midst of the elders, stood a Lamb as it had been slain...* (Revelation 5:6).

Notice they are worshiping the Lamb *as it had been slain*. In other words, just like the first part of my vision, they are seeing the crucified Savior, bloodied and broken; they are acknowledging Him in that condition as He had been slain! We need to understand the cross and what Jesus accomplished by dying upon it. In this verse, Heaven was getting a revelation of the Lamb as slain. We need to know Jesus not only in the fellowship of His sufferings, but also in the power of His resurrection (see Phil. 3:10).

The next reference to the Lamb is found in Revelation 5:12: *"Worthy is the Lamb that was slain to receive power, and riches, and wisdom, and strength, and honour, and glory, and blessing."* He is now being worshiped as the slain Lamb that is worthy, resurrected, and enthroned as the Lord of all.

This double revelation is crucial to our understanding of Jesus; we must know Him both as the Lamb crucified and as the Lamb resurrected in Heaven for all to worship. How simple, how profound— the Lamb slain for our sins: *our Savior;* and the Lamb resurrected for our earthly blessings and eternal salvation: *our Lord.*

Think back for a moment to the Exodus account of the Passover lamb: if blood from a lamb could save and protect the Jewish nation on the night of the first Passover meal, then how much more can the Lamb of God save and protect? We can partake of a personal relationship with Jesus and be saved and protected through what He provided by shedding His blood as the slain Lamb of God. Remarkably, it doesn't stop there; we can hold onto this same promise and see those we love come under the same protection! He is the Lamb provided for all; we just need to be the ones willing to share Him with everyone we meet. I hope you are getting such a revelation of God's love for you, for families, and for all people; the proof is that He gave His Son as a Lamb!

THE GOD OF HOUSEHOLD SALVATION

By now you should understand how important the salvation of your whole family is to Him. He wants to reach *every* household, and He longs to add more households to the family both in Heaven and on earth. In fact, God sees our relatives in Heaven and those of us here on earth as one big household, or family! Jesus revealed that God is a God of households and that His desire is for them to be saved when He called Heaven His Father's house (see John 14:2).

The apostle Paul referred to God's household in his prayers for the church of Ephesus: *"For this cause I bow my knees unto the Father of our Lord Jesus Christ, of whom the whole family in heaven and earth* is named" (Eph. 3:14-15). In Scripture, the Church is called the "*household of faith*" (Gal. 6:10). God is the God of the family.

Let's take a moment to look at how much God values the family in Scripture. As mentioned earlier, we know the first family or household unit on earth was established by God when He created Adam and Eve. It was the Lord who said it was not good for Adam to be alone, giving him a helpmate for love, companionship, partnership, and fruitfulness in the earth. He instructed them to establish a family, to be fruitful and multiply (see Gen. 1:26-28).

In the Old Testament, God often uses family descriptions such as the "house of Jacob" or the "house of Israel"; He refers to Abraham as the "father of many nations." Furthermore, God thinks generationally and in terms of families—for example, "*This is the book of the generations of Adam*" (Gen. 5:1); "*These are the generations of Noah*" (Gen. 6:9); "*Come thou and all thy house into the ark*" (Gen. 7:1).

God is the God of households, generations, and nations; He thinks in these terms. Think of it this way: when one person gets saved, it opens the way for the whole family to follow. Our family members are not automatically saved just because one individual in the family is, but that initial salvation does position the family for the promise of household salvation through Jesus the Lamb of God! That household can impact the whole generational line, and throughout the generations that follow, people who come into the household of faith will be affecting communities, cities, and nations for the Lord.

When you study the many examples of household salvations in Scripture, it is amazing to see just how much God wants families saved:

- Noah built an ark to save his family: "*By faith Noah, being warned of God of things not seen as yet, moved with fear, prepared an ark to the saving of his house*" (Heb. 11:7).

- Joseph helped preserve his family in famine: "*And God sent me before you to preserve you a posterity in the earth, and to save your lives by a great deliverance*" (Gen. 45:7); "*And take your father and your households, and come unto me…*" (Gen. 45:18).

- Moses received direction that helped save every Israelite household: "*…they shall take to them every man a lamb, according to the house of their fathers, a lamb for an house*" (Exod. 12:3).

- Rahab the harlot saved her house: "*…shew kindness unto my father's house, and give me a true token: And that ye will save alive my father, and my mother, and my brethren, and my sisters, and all that they have, and deliver our lives from death*" (Josh. 2:12-13).

- Joshua determined that his whole house would serve the Lord: "*And if it seem evil unto you to serve the LORD, choose you this day whom ye will serve; whether the gods which your fathers served that were on the other side of the flood, or the gods of the Amorites, in whose land ye dwell: but as for me and my house, we will serve the LORD*" (Josh. 24:15).

There are even more examples of household salvations and families being blessed by God in the New Testament. For instance, Jesus told Zacchaeus (a tax collector who climbed a tree to get a better glimpse of the Lord) that salvation had come to his whole household (see Luke 19:9). Salvation did not come to Zacchaeus alone, but to his whole house. The same is true for me and you. On another occasion, Jesus healed a nobleman's son who was dying, resulting in the *whole house* being saved (see John 4:53). The book of Acts gives us even more examples of entire households being saved.

- The Household of Cornelius: Cornelius was *"devout... and one that feared God with all his house, which gave much alms to the people, and prayed to God alway"* (Acts 10:2). Acts 11:14 says that Cornelius saw an angel who said that Peter would come and *"tell you words by which you and all your household will be saved"* (NKJV). Cornelius's entire household was saved; it was not Cornelius alone. Cornelius invited his relatives and close friends to hear the words of Peter.

- The Household of Lydia: Acts 16:15 says, *"...she was baptized, and her household."* The apostle Paul preached the Gospel to Lydia's household, and the whole household believed and was baptized.

- The Household of the Jailer: Acts 16:31 says, *"Believe on the Lord Jesus Christ, and you will be saved, you and your household"* (NKJV). Later, the jailer brought his household to Paul. After Paul spoke to them, they believed and were even baptized.

- The Household of Crispus: Acts 18:8 says, *"Crispus, the ruler of the synagogue, believed on the Lord with all his household...and were baptized"* (NKJV).

I pray that these examples of household salvations ignite your faith to believe for every one of your family members to be saved! This is what God wants, and so should we. Why should we believe for our entire household? Because if we just believe for one person or only for ourselves, then that will be the result. But if we dare to believe for our whole family, as we have seen in these scriptural examples, then our entire families can be saved and for generations

after! We must think like God does—in terms of family and generations! If we will connect our faith with God's desire for our families
to be saved, we will be amazed at the results.

COME YOU AND ALL YOUR HOUSE

Perhaps you might be thinking that your family is a particularly
hard case, nearly impossible, while others might be praying, "Lord,
will You really save my family?" God's answer is yes; He can save
our families if we will continue to pray and believe. Certainly, people's wills are involved in making a decision to accept the Lord, but
having revelation of household salvation coupled with prayer can
produce what may seem impossible. It can bring laborers into our
family's lives, soften them for the Gospel, and ready them to receive
the Lord.

The Lord had an entire family on His mind when He spoke
to Noah about building an ark. God knew that only Noah would
believe, and He instructed him to prepare a way of escape. It was
God's idea: *"But I will establish My covenant with you, and you will enter
the ark—you and your sons and your wife and your sons' wives with you"*
(Gen. 6:18 NIV).

Be encouraged that if God wanted this for Noah, then He certainly wants this for you and your family. What is even more faith
building and amazing is that the first "invitation" given in the Bible
was for the saving of a family. You might say that this was the very
first altar call ever given; God gave it, and the result was the salvation of a whole family! *"And the LORD said unto Noah, Come thou
and all thy house into the ark; for thee have I seen righteous before me in
this generation"* (Gen. 7:1). Every member of Noah's family was saved
in that ark: eight people altogether, including those related to Noah
through marriage.

Yes, that's right—even those wonderful in-laws that some may love to hate and others want to avoid and forget. For Noah, this meant his daughters-in-law, but for you it may be another "in-law" or relative; the key thing to remember is that God wants them all saved, as was the case with Noah and his family:

> *In the selfsame day entered Noah, and Shem, and Ham, and Japheth, the sons of Noah, and Noah's wife, and the three wives of his sons with them, into the ark* (Genesis 7:13).

Another indication of how much God wants our entire households saved is by an unusual instruction given to Noah. God told him to cover the ark with "pitch" both inside and outside: *"Make thee an ark of gopher wood; rooms shalt thou make in the ark, and shalt pitch it within and without with pitch"* (Gen. 6:14). You could say that Noah threw the first "pitch" in the "beginning" of time. But seriously, what this pitch represents is a powerful truth regarding households saved through the blood of Jesus. The pitch was most likely some type of tar, or glue, that held the ark together making it waterproof. The Hebrew word for pitch is *kaphar*, meaning to cover, appease, make atonement, cleanse, disannul, forgive, be merciful, pacify, and pardon.[1]

As you can see, the Hebrew word for pitch is also the same word as *atonement*. Why is this important? Because Jesus' blood made a covering, or *atoning*, of our sins; in fact, His blood shed on Calvary didn't just cover our sins, it completely did away with them! *"Blotting out the handwriting of ordinances that was against us, which was contrary to us, and took it out of the way, nailing it to his cross"* (Col. 2:14). This act enables us as humans to be reconciled to God, to be justified, forgiven, and made righteous in His sight.

We may also prophetically compare the ark of wood covered with pitch and the wooden cross of Calvary: both the ark of Noah and the cross of Christ provided salvation for whole households! Furthermore, the ark of Noah uniquely contained only one door: *"...and the door of the ark shalt thou set in the side thereof"* (Gen. 6:16). Why is that relevant? Because the only way to be saved in the day of Noah was through the door of the ark, and the only way to salvation in Heaven is through Jesus who said He was the door! *"I am the door. If anyone enters by Me, he will be saved, and will go in and out and find pasture"* (John 10:9 NKJV). No man, no family, no household can be saved without coming to the door, Jesus. We have the promise of salvation *only* through Him.

TWO POWERFUL PROMISES

Through Jesus we have access to many promises if we will believe and receive them. There are two very powerful promises, of the many that the Lord has provided, that we can claim individually and for our families also. We find these two promises in Acts 16, when Paul and Silas were thrown into jail and had a supernatural encounter with a jailer. They were worshiping in their cell when the Lord caused an earthquake to shake the prison. This was such a supernatural intervention of God that the jailer assigned to Paul and Silas was visibly shaken. He feared that the prisoners in his charge had escaped. Just as the jailer was about to kill himself, Paul called out to him, letting him know that every prisoner in the prison was accounted for. Paul and Silas then gave this jailer two promises that not only affected the jailer but also his household: *"They replied, "Believe in the Lord Jesus and you will be saved, along with everyone in your household""* (Acts 16:31 NLT). The first promise was for the jailer's salvation if he would believe in the Lord Jesus. The second promise was for the saving of his family if they would believe also!

Too often we view salvation as something that is available to the individual only. We know the devil doesn't want us to claim, pray, and believe for the first promise—and he certainly doesn't want us to claim the second promise for our families either. He wants to keep us uninformed of the second promise given to the jailer regarding his household because it affects more lives. We must believe for our families! As this book has clearly set out, salvation is available for your family, your entire household. Can you imagine what would happen if more Christians came to the understanding that God wants their entire households saved? We would see more people coming to the Lord and more people in our families coming to know Him. This promise was given to the jailer and his house, and it is available to you. Paul wasn't offering something that couldn't be delivered—that would misrepresent God and His promises. He fully understood that God is the God who saves families and wants us to believe for their salvation!

God will fulfill His promises, and He can be trusted. We have a promise of salvation for us and our families. We need to trust Him and thank God for this promise. It is available to us today; we just need to position ourselves to receive through prayer and faith.

In Acts 1, the Holy Spirit came and filled the 120 who were gathered in the Upper Room. He didn't come just because they were in one mind and one accord. The main reason the Holy Spirit came was because Jesus promised that He would!

> *And, being assembled together with them, commanded them that they should not depart from Jerusalem, but wait for the promise of the Father...* (Acts 1:4).

We know God promised salvation through His Son Jesus to anyone who would receive it (see John 3:16).

God will fulfill His promises in our lives if we will believe it. We need to get in position to receive these promises for our loved ones to be saved. We can't give up until we see the promise of them saved and watch them come in one by one by one! If the first part of the promise of our salvation works when received by faith, then the second part of the promise of our family being saved is equally possible!

Let these two promises really sink into your heart so you claim this same promise over your families no matter how hopeless or sinful their lives may be. God wants to bless and reach families, and that means yours! Remember, this promise was not for just the jailer individually, but for his entire household. Your salvation isn't just for you to enjoy, celebrate, and glory in; it is also for your family to experience. Let's start believing for our families!

Remember, our faith helps to position them for salvation, but it is still, ultimately, an individual decision for each of them. In other words, they are not automatically saved just because we have been. What our faith does is open the way for God to reach them and for their hearts to be open to the Gospel. Remember, there are two promises: one promise for you, and the other for your family! Our responsibility is to believe in the Lord unto salvation and then believe for our households to follow. This was how it worked for the jailer and his household. The jailer had to believe first, receiving the first promise of salvation:

> And brought them out, and said, Sirs, what must I do to
> be saved? And they said, Believe on the Lord Jesus Christ,
> and thou shalt be saved, and thy house (Acts 16:30-31).

His household had to hear the Gospel and believe for themselves: "And they spake unto him the word of the Lord, and to all that were in his house" (Acts 16:32). When the jailer's family heard the Word of the

Lord, they believed, resulting in the whole household being saved: "*And when he had brought them into his house, he set meat before them, and rejoiced, believing in God with all his house*" (Acts 16:34). Clearly, salvation didn't happen automatically for the family—but the jailer's salvation and the Gospel preached to his family opened the way. God wants everyone—you could say—*all in the family* saved!

ALL IN THE FAMILY

I want to share some final examples to encourage you before we end this chapter. We need to remember how much God values one soul. As discussed in the stories in Chapter Two—stories Jesus told of the lost sheep, the lost coin, and the prodigal son in Luke 15. I want to revisit these stories, but this time I want to look at them from the perspective of God's desire for the salvation of households.

Luke 15 begins with Jesus ministering to sinners; the scribes and Pharisees are not happy about it and begin to talk against Him: "*And the Pharisees and scribes murmured, saying, This man receiveth sinners, and eateth with them*" (Luke 15:2). The Lord responds to these murmuring religious leaders by telling three stories about someone or something that has been lost. In the first story, a sheepfold has lost a sheep; in the second story, a woman has lost a coin in her house; and in the third story, Jesus tells of the prodigal son, a family member, lost and separated from the rest of the house. In each of these three examples, the sheepfold or house was not complete, *or didn't fully rejoice*, until what was lost had finally been found: "*Rejoice with me; for I have found my sheep which was lost*" (Luke 15:6); "*Rejoice with me; for I have found the piece which I had lost*" (Luke 15:9); "*It was meet that we should make merry, and be glad: for this thy brother was dead, and is alive again; and was lost, and is found*" (Luke 15:32).

In the first story, Jesus speaks about one lost sheep that wanders off from the rest of the sheepfold or family. I believe this parable speaks of not only individual salvation, but also of those already saved in the house or sheepfold. How can we see this? Well, Jesus speaks of a shepherd who has one hundred sheep; the shepherd leaves the other ninety-nine sheep, that aren't lost, to seek the one that is: *"What man of you, having an hundred sheep, if he lose one of them, doth not leave the ninety and nine in the wilderness, and go after that which is lost, until he find it?"* (Luke 15:4).

While this story certainly does point to the value of each soul and individual salvation, the story doesn't stop there; it also references the whole household. You see, the other ninety-nine sheep weren't lost in the sheepfold/household. The only one lost was the one sheep the shepherd went looking for; once he found it, he brought it home to the other ninety-nine who weren't lost. Do you see it? Now not *one* sheep is lost in the *whole* sheepfold or household—the entire household is accounted for! The shepherd wants to see all of the "family" saved and rejoices in this: *"And when he cometh home, he calleth together his friends and neighbours, saying unto them, Rejoice with me; for I have found my sheep which was lost"* (Luke 15:6).

Again, this sheep represented a lost soul from the sheepfold, or family. The lost sheep was the only one that wasn't saved in the sheepfold because he was out wandering, lost and unprotected. This sheep had to be saved and returned to the sheepfold, which represents the household. We know that it represents a lost family member because of what Jesus said upon the return of this sheep to the sheepfold: *"I say unto you, that likewise joy shall be in heaven over one sinner that repenteth, more than over ninety and nine just persons, which need no repentance"* (Luke 15:7). According to this verse, the other ninety-nine sheep in the sheepfold or household didn't need to be saved because Jesus called them "just." The only one who needed to repent was this last, lost sheep. Now the whole family is saved and accounted for!

Next, Jesus shares a story about a coin that was lost in a house. This story also clearly illustrates both of the promises we have read about in this chapter. The one coin that was lost represents a lost soul like the lost sheep in the first story. That the coin was lost in the house speaks to us of both individual (coin) and household (house) salvation. The story points to household salvation because the coin was something in the house that was lost:

> *Either what woman having ten pieces of silver, if she lose one piece, doth not light a candle, and sweep the house, and seek diligently till she find it?* (Luke 15:8)

Jesus' love and desire for our families to be saved is illustrated by the desperate way the woman is looking through her house to find the lost coin. The woman lights a candle and diligently seeks to find the lost coin that represents an individual; the other nine coins, which were accounted for, represent household salvation. You see, the house is not complete until this lost coin is found and accounted for with the other nine pieces!

Jesus then tells the third story, the well-known parable of the prodigal son. Yet, what is often not mentioned in Sunday school classes, books, or sermons is that this parable is not just about a rebellious son who is saved; it is about a household that is made complete. How the father rejoices when his lost son is home—saved and accounted for! He throws a lavish party of welcome:

> *For this my son was dead, and is alive again; he was lost, and is found. And they began to be merry. Now his elder*

son was in the field: and as he came and drew nigh to the house, he heard musick and dancing" (Luke 15:24-25).

The house of this father was not complete until this prodigal came home, just as the house was incomplete until the lost sheep and lost coin were accounted for. It was the father's desire in this story, as it is also our heavenly Father's desire, for every one of the family members to be saved. It doesn't matter what they have done, God, our Father—like the prodigal's father—will accept them, love them, and forgive them if they will come to Him.

We all need to reexamine our hearts and our approach to our families being saved. This means in-laws and outlaws. *All in the family*—God wants every one of them saved!

What is your heart and approach toward your family members being saved—or even toward winning the lost?

We can learn a serious lesson that will cause us to check our own hearts by looking at the elder son, in the story of the prodigal, and his attitude toward his brother. He became angry and was more concerned about his life, his comfort, and his blessings than he was about a lost soul, specifically his brother:

> And [the servant] *said unto him, Thy brother is come; and thy father hath killed the fatted calf, because he hath received him safe and sound. And he was angry, and would not go in: therefore came his father out, and intreated him. And he answering said to his father, Lo, these many years do I serve thee, neither transgressed I at any time thy commandment: and yet thou never gavest me a kid, that I might make merry with my friends: But as soon as this thy son was come...* (Luke 15:27-30).

Unfortunately, many approach winning souls or reaching their own family with the Gospel with a similar attitude. They are living their lives to the fullest, enjoying their own comfort and blessings, but they are not concerned about their families or others being saved. We must not be like this elder son in this regard. We need to love lost souls and believe for others, *especially* our family, as Jesus showed us in these three parables.

I want to encourage you right now to begin to call out to God, believing for your entire household to be saved. Remember the request of the rich man in hell? He wanted his brothers saved! Let's continue to stand and believe for the salvation of our families. God wants this, and I know deep in your heart that is your desire too. Perhaps your family is already saved. If that's the case, then you can stand praying and believing for other families.

Whether we believe for our own family, or someone else's, let's take a moment to pray together for them right now. Let's claim these two promises that were spoken to the jailer in Acts 16:31: *"Believe on the Lord Jesus Christ, and thou shalt be saved, and thy house."* Are you ready? Let's pray!

> Dear heavenly Father, first of all, I receive the promise of salvation for my life. I believe in my heart that You raised Jesus from the dead. I now say with my mouth that Jesus is Lord. The Bible says that whoever calls on the name of the Lord will be saved. I call on Jesus to come and save me, forgive me of my sins, and be the Lord of my life.
>
> I now pray for my family and for others who have family members who don't know the Lord. I ask You, God, to bring people into their lives so they can be saved. Soften their hearts; create opportunities for

them to hear and receive the Gospel. I ask, Lord, that You keep the devil from hindering their lives or their decision to come to You. We claim the promise of household salvation and believe, declaring that it is working in their lives at this moment.

Now mention their names, under your breath, in your heart, or out loud to God! Don't stop believing and calling out to God for them. You will see in the next chapter more ways to reach our families, loved ones, and others for the Gospel. It is never too late, and I believe the time is now for salvation!

ENDNOTE

1. *Kaphar*; see http://concordances.org/hebrew/3722.htm.

Chapter Five

HOW TO REACH YOUR FAMILY AND OTHERS

By faith Noah, being warned of God of things not seen

as yet, moved with fear, prepared an ark to the saving

of his house; by the which he condemned the world,

and became heir of the righteousness which is by faith

(Hebrews 11:7).

"I have decided it's time to go," were the last words I remember saying as I drove away from my parents' home. I had given my life to Jesus shortly after I graduated from high school, and I was so excited about my newly found relationship with the Lord that I became insensitive to my family. I spent countless hours away from home dedicated to the church I was attending, which was different from the one my family had attended for years. I also made nearly every moment my soapbox preaching opportunity to give the Gospel to my parents. I was literally shoving it down their throats with what was sometimes an unwise zeal for the Lord.

When it became necessary to move out of my parents' home, I began alienating myself from my family. Tensions grew between us to the point that we had little to no contact. I quit caring as much whether they would come to know the Lord in the way I had come to know and love Him. I even started to harden my heart as to whether they went to Heaven or hell. I was moving on in my zealous Christian faith but was forgetting my family.

Looking back now, over 25 years later, I know this was not wise, but God has mercifully done amazing things since then to strengthen our family relationships. We talk openly and respectfully about the things of God today.

What happened to change this? My willingness to get my heart right and really pray for my family members played a big part in the salvations that have taken place in my family. I had to realize the power of praying for my family and the power of the "household blessing." What do I mean by "household blessing"? Simply that God wants our families not only saved, but unified, blessed, and at peace with Him and each other. For me, in order for this to happen, there were some things that I had to do!

THE HOUSEHOLD BLESSING — BLESSING OUR FAMILIES!

I had failed to realize, in my new Christian zeal, how much the Lord values our families being blessed and saved. So I didn't pray for my family as much as I should have in those days, and I didn't use wisdom or sensitivity in reaching them. All too often believers make these same mistakes when trying to reach their families or others for the Gospel. God wants to bless our households; that is a given, yet it is important to know how and when to reach them.

Once we have come to the revelation of how much God wants our households blessed, we are empowered with a spirit of faith to believe for our loved ones. God wants them all saved and walking in His peace. He doesn't want strife, contention, unforgiveness, or any other thing to interfere with His blessing. The greatest blessing the Lord gives to a household is salvation.

In this chapter, I want you to see how much God wants households blessed. I want you to discover ways to reach your family that will save you both headaches and heartaches. Be encouraged by just how much God wants your family saved and blessed. In fact, He wants it more than we do! We need to start blessing our family members—whether they are saved already or still need to give their lives to the Lord.

It is so important with our families not to be overbearing, mean, unforgiving, offended, or callous about whether they go to Heaven or not. We need to speak blessings over and to our families. When we do this, they are positioned for blessings and opportunities to get saved; one of the first things God did when He created Adam was to bless him (see Gen. 1:28).

It is too easy to let the devil deceive us into thinking our prayers aren't working or that our loved ones are too far gone to change. Don't give up; you may be the very one who makes the difference even though your family is not serving God. Have you ever thought about the fact that the Bible never says that Noah's family was righteous? Genesis 6:9 says only that *"Noah was a just man and perfect in his generations"*—but in the end, his entire family was saved in the ark: *"Then the LORD said to Noah, "Enter the ark, you and all your household, for you alone I have seen to be righteous before Me in this time"* (Gen. 7:1 NASB).

Day by day, month by month, and year by year, Noah kept building the ark, believing for his family to be saved with him. We don't know exactly how long it took to build, but it's possible that it was close to one hundred years (see Gen. 5:32; 7:6). At any rate, enough time had elapsed for his three sons to grow up and have wives. He didn't exclude his family as he prepared the ark. He had his family in mind. Over time, Noah's lifestyle of righteousness and his obedience to the Lord was a testimony to his family; eventually, they were convinced to join him in the ark: *"…to those who were disobedient long ago when God waited patiently in the days of Noah while the ark was being built. In it only a few people, eight in all, were saved through water"* (1 Pet. 3:20 NIV).

Only eight people were saved from among those who dwelt on the earth because of the righteous lifestyle and actions of Noah. If we keep serving the Lord, living righteously and honorably with a Christian testimony, the same will be true for us. If we will remain faithful and pray, God can save our families as He saved Noah's family in the ark. We need to be the righteous ones, like Noah, who invite and bring our loved ones into the ark—which speaks of the Kingdom of God today. Never forget how much God wants to bless your household.

Household blessings were so important to Jesus that He instructed His disciples when they entered a home to bless it! *"Whenever you enter someone's home, first say, 'May God's peace be on this house.' If those who live there are peaceful, the blessing will stand; if they are not, the blessing will return to you"* (Luke 10:5-6 NLT). Jesus' instruction didn't pertain only to blessing an individual in the house; the whole house was to be blessed! How awesome to see God's desire to bless and reach our households and entire families! So keep praying for them and declaring blessing and peace upon them!

We also find that God's blessing was given to an entire household in the days of Obed-Edom. His whole family was blessed as a result of God's presence. Second Samuel 6:11 says, *"And the ark of the LORD continued in the house of Obededom the Gittite three months: and the LORD blessed Obededom, and all his household."*

Even the covenant that God made with Abraham was not just for him individually but for his whole household and the generations that followed. The household blessing that God extended to Abraham was marked by circumcision as a sign of a covenant between God, Abraham, and his household for generations to come. Circumcision was required for all of the men born into his house (see Gen. 17:12-13). Circumcision was a dividing line between those who were covenanted to God and those who weren't; it was a sign of the whole family being saved and blessed under the covenant of God. We too can pray and see our families blessed when we accept Jesus as our Lord. Salvation releases the promises of God to us and to our families, positioning them for salvation and blessing!

A SEED FOR A FAMILY

You see, it only takes one person in a family, as an initial seed, to bring the harvest of the rest of the family to the Lord. For example, I was one of the first in my family to make a decision to serve, love, and commit my whole life to the Lord Jesus. Since that decision over two decades ago, others in my family have come to know the Lord. I am convinced that my life and decision was a spiritual seed that helped unlock the way of salvation for other family members. As I've mentioned, in the early years of my Christianity, I turned my family off to the Gospel more than I got them excited. I spent many hours overzealously trying to convince them to accept Jesus as their Lord; I was often preachy and pushy, getting into some very heated arguments that produced no fruit. I have learned that it is far more beneficial when our new lives in Christ speak louder than our words.

It is helpful to ask the Lord for His wisdom and direction in reaching our families. I want you to get excited and plant a seed of faith in your own heart to believe for them to be blessed and saved! Something very powerful happens when one person gets saved in a family; it opens the way for the rest of the family to know the Lord. Let's look at some scriptural examples that we can claim as promises for our own families, beginning with the story of Noah.

Religion has taught us, through Sunday school classes and in different songs about the ark, that the focus of the Noah account is the animals and the flood. In fact, Noah built the ark to save his family—not just to save the animals from the flood. That was his real focus and main purpose: *"By faith Noah, being warned of God of things not seen as yet, moved with fear, prepared an ark to the saving of his house…"* (Heb. 11:7). Building the ark was God's idea—to save Noah and his family first, then the animals to follow. Yet, the responsibility to save Noah's family was not God's alone, but also Noah's! He spent years preparing the ark to save his family. The same is true for you and me today!

Obviously, this doesn't mean we should start building an actual boat in our back yards. But God wants our families to be saved, and it's up to us, as members of the family, to prepare the opportunity for them. Just as Noah had to build the ark piece by piece, hammering and sawing by the sweat of his brow, we need to work at building a spiritual ark by our prayers, love, and a godly, consistent Christian lifestyle lived openly before our family and loved ones. Building a spiritual ark does *not* imply acting self-righteously, beating family members over the head with the Bible, or berating them with the Gospel. I did this to my family when I first got saved and found that it did more harm than good. Rather, we need to demonstrate God's love, pray for them, and share the Gospel when it is appropriate. We also need to ask the Lord to send people into their lives to share the Gospel and be a godly witness.

When you build a spiritual ark, you are preparing and believing for God to save your family or others; God then adds His faith to your faith, and His action to your action to reach your family. How do we know this? Let's look at a verse in Scripture where an interesting reference to Noah is found: *"And spared not the old world, but saved Noah the eighth person, a preacher of righteousness, bringing in the flood upon the world of the ungodly"* (2 Pet. 2:5).

Here it says, "Noah the *eighth* person." However, Genesis 7:13 shows that there were eight people who entered the ark and lists Noah as entering *first*: *"In the selfsame day entered Noah, and Shem, and Ham, and Japheth, the sons of Noah, and Noah's wife, and the three wives of his sons with them, into the ark."*

As this verse indicates, normally, the head of household or the eldest family member is listed first. In the natural, that is because they provided the seed of life for the entire family. This offers some prophetic insight into household salvations: spiritually speaking, a "first" person could be the first one saved in a family, a forerunner or seed of salvation for the remaining family members.

So, if Noah was first, then why does Second Peter call him the eighth person? With eight people entering the ark, that designation would make Noah the very last. As the head of the family and the first righteous person (or you might say the first one "saved"), he is now being described as the eighth, which offers a key revelation. I believe it shows that now, through the blood of Christ, the family members who entered before him were already considered "saved" under his umbrella of righteousness or salvation!

Does this mean that God automatically includes your family if you are saved? No, but this passage reveals that you are not only the "first" powerful seed that will present the Gospel to your family, but also that God wants you to see your family responding to your seed of decision to follow Christ and coming under the umbrella of your salvation experience. God wants us to see that, through the blood of Jesus, He is seeing our families saved by faith. What a picture of God adding faith to our faith!

Another biblical example is found in the story of Rahab the harlot, who asked for the salvation of her household. Her request of faith for her family to be saved provided that opportunity for her family:

> And Joshua saved Rahab the harlot alive, and her father's household, and all that she had; and she dwelleth in Israel even unto this day; because she hid the messengers, which Joshua sent to spy out Jericho (Joshua 6:25).

Rahab's entire house was spared by a scarlet thread, representing the saving blood of Jesus that was used to save her household. Her family came under an umbrella that not only saved her but her whole household!

> Behold, when we come into the land, thou shalt bind this line of scarlet thread in the window which thou didst let us down by: and thou shalt bring thy father, and thy mother, and thy brethren, and all thy father's household, home unto thee (Joshua 2:18).

Rahab had to claim the promise that everyone in her family would be saved if she would hang the scarlet thread from the window. We have the same promise of salvation through the blood of Jesus to which we may cling for our loved ones. All it took was for Rahab to stand up for her whole family to position them to be blessed and saved. Like Noah, she made preparations to save her household. Not only was her family saved, but she became part of the lineage of Jesus! (See Matthew 1:5.) We need to be like Rahab and Noah, making preparations for the salvation of our families and boldly exercising faith, love, and action on their behalf.

As we pray for our families to be saved, we must also make sure that we use Spirit-led methods, wisdom, and timing in reaching them. If we don't, we can hinder them from coming to know the Lord.

This was exactly the case with a certain woman years ago, who by the request of her pastor invited my wife, Brenda, and me to speak to her husband. We reluctantly agreed to meet with him, unsure of what we would encounter. The wife gave us a brief rundown of the situation: her husband refused to accept Jesus and wouldn't commit to attending church with her. Instead, he would get angry and drunk. She was frustrated with him, his outbursts of anger, and his dissatisfaction with her church involvement.

As we entered the house, I saw an older man who looked pretty determined not to accept Jesus into his life or attend church. We began to visit, looking for an opportunity to minister to him. He eventually asked if he could play us a song on his ukulele. My wife and I agreed, and he began to play, while singing off tune, the song called, "Little Brown Jug." My wife and I just smiled while he continued his proud concert. I think a couple of cats started screeching and a few dogs were howling in the alley as the sound pierced their ears and ours.

We were so thankful when he stopped—but I could see he was playing with all his heart. At that moment I asked him why he hadn't accepted Jesus in his life or gone to church with his wife. He looked up at me and asked, "Would you go to church if your house looked like this? Look at this place; it's awful! I hardly ever get a hot meal because my wife is always running to that church doing something while I stay at home in this mess!" He felt his needs were being neglected while the church was getting his wife's entire attention. As a result, it was hindering him from coming to the Lord or going to church. He wasn't interested in anything she had to say until she cleaned the filthy house and made him feel that he was important.

This woman should have, like Noah, prepared an ark—or a house—that her family might be saved. What do I mean? By taking the time to keep her home clean and look after the needs of her husband more than her church, she would have helped prepare his heart to be saved. Her actions would have been a testimony of God's goodness and love. We can make our ark more appealing to our families, first of all, by not bashing them over the head with a Gospel two-by-four. Second, we need to keep praying and showing acts of kindness and love, not ignoring our everyday responsibilities. For example, the apostle Peter speaks of how a saved woman can reach her unsaved husband:

> In the same way, you wives must accept the authority of your husbands. Then, even if some refuse to obey the Good News, your godly lives will speak to them without any words. They will be won over by observing your pure and reverent lives (1 Peter 3:1-2 NLT).

Notice that this verse puts a strong emphasis on our actions as well as the Gospel message. Let us not be like the woman who wanted her husband saved, but was hindering his salvation by unwise behavior. Remember, he who is wise wins souls (see Prov. 11:30). We need to be wise when it comes to reaching people, especially our family members and those who really know us. Because they are more familiar with us, it's often harder to convince them that there has been a genuine change in our lives. We can end up overcompensating and overevangelizing. In the end, we have to pray and be wise, remembering that the devil is holding their lives captive—but we have a Savior who can set them free!

THE LAWFUL CAPTIVE DELIVERED

We need to prepare a spiritual ark like Noah or take a step of faith like Rahab because the devil wants to hold our relatives and loved ones captive. The Bible calls the devil the god of this world who has spiritually blinded the minds of people, keeping them from the knowledge of the truth (see 2 Cor. 4:4). The devil doesn't want people saved, especially our loved ones. As long as they are not saved, he has a legal, spiritual hold upon them that requires the Gospel message and the power of Jesus to set them free. The Bible says in Isaiah 49:24, *"Shall the prey be taken from the mighty, or the lawful captive delivered?"* This verse asks whether those who are held in the hands of the devil as prey, or those he has a legal hold on as lawful captives, will ever be delivered. What does this mean? It means that our family, friends, loved ones, relatives, and everyone born into this world are held in captivity lawfully because of sin.

How did this happen? When Adam and Eve sinned in the Garden, they gave the devil a legal right to hold humankind captive. Until a person is saved, he is the prey and lawful captive of Satan, held captive by him under the power of sin. When a believer calls on the name of the Lord to be saved, the legal right of Satan is broken. The devil will continue to hold our families, loved ones, friends, and all humankind under his demonic legal control until they are delivered through the power of the cross of Jesus. This does not mean we are without hope. On the contrary, because of Jesus' shed blood and the power of His resurrection, those who turn to Christ now have victory and are delivered from Satan's legal hold.

Preparing a spiritual ark, like Noah, and claiming the promises through the blood of Jesus, like Rahab, can position our families for salvation, blessing, and freedom from the stronghold of the devil. When we become determined to see our families saved like Noah and Rahab, then God gets involved and sets them free:

> Thus saith the LORD, Even the captives of the mighty shall be taken away, and the prey of the terrible shall be delivered: for I will contend with him that contends with thee, and I will save thy children (Isaiah 49:25).

This verse says that it is God who takes away from the devil, referred to as the "mighty and terrible," those held legally captive through sin and delivers them—and that includes our children!

Once when I was preaching near the border of Mexico, the pastor I was ministering for invited me to go to a Mexican prison where he had an outreach. I was absolutely unprepared for what I saw there. Talk about people being held captive! I have ministered in jails before, but never anything of this magnitude. I will never forget the smell, the cells open to the elements, the oppressive demonic presence, or the sound of those held captive. The prison guard led me to an open court that was in the middle of all the prison cells. There were cells on every side of me at least three to four stories high. Some of the prisoners were hanging their heads and hands out of the bars yelling while others just walked about. To me, it was like looking at an earthly hell. When I took the microphone to speak, they tried to drown out my preaching with their yelling. I kept preaching until I eventually told everyone to be quiet; I couldn't believe what I had just said. I thought, *Hank, you need to be wise here because these prisoners outnumber you.* Yet, I felt such a strong presence of God protecting me, and such strength in my words.

I continued to preach as the noise quieted immensely until I gave the invitation to be saved, healed, and delivered. A group of prisoners came forward for prayer, and what happened next caught me by surprise. A young man with sunglasses reached up, grabbed my hand, and in perfect English asked me to help him. I replied, "You speak great English!" He said, "That's right; I am an American citizen who was thrown in this hell for over six months. They have forgotten about me in here and thrown away the key. Will you please go and tell my family that I am being held captive unlawfully?

"Please," he said, "my parents don't know I am here. They are Christians, and I know they are praying for me. I have been running from Jesus and the truth. My parents pray for me all the time, but I have yet to accept the Lord. I want to now; will you pray with me?"

I prayed for him and with him. After I left, the pastor I was with made sure that follow up with that man's family was being attempted.

Think about it for a moment: his family was praying for him, and he was held as a captive in prison. To me, this situation perfectly exemplifies the verse from Isaiah 49:25: God will deliver us, our children, and those held captive by the enemy. When we pray, captives can be set free! I am convinced that had the family not prayed for him, this man could have been lost in that horrible prison. We must never give up on our loved ones—so many are held captive in a prison of sin, bound by the devil.

If we are saved, then it is our responsibility to pray so our loved ones can be delivered from the grip of sin and the power of the devil, like this man in the Mexican prison. We need to be determined, as Joshua was over his family, that they will serve the Lord: "*As for me and my house, we will serve the LORD"* (Josh. 24:15). We need to rise up and bind the enemy from our families and loved ones' lives. Jesus showed us the power we have to see our families saved by binding the strong man over our families. This means we are to spiritually address the devil through prayer, commanding him to take his hands off our families and loved ones. We need to continue to bind the works of darkness that try to influence and hold them spiritually captive in the grips of sin:

> *But if I am casting out demons by the power of God, then the Kingdom of God has arrived among you. For when a strong man like Satan is fully armed and guards his palace, his possessions are safe* (Luke 11:20-21 NLT).

This verse shows us that as long as the devil is unchallenged by our lack of prayer or testimony, then his goods (people and other things in his possession) remain untouched. We must rise up with the authority of Jesus and in His name pray and preach the Gospel to them. When we use our authority, we undo the power of the enemy and set people free. As Christians, we are the stronger ones through Jesus' power and the Gospel:

> *But when a stronger than he shall come upon him, and overcome him, he taketh from him all his armour wherein he trusted, and divideth his spoils* (Luke 11:22).

Once the devil is cast out, his power is broken over our lives and families. This positions them to hear the Gospel and receive it. This is why Jesus tells us that we must first bind the strongman and then spoil his house—so people will be free from Satan's hold:

Or else how can one enter into a strong man's house, and spoil his goods, except he first bind the strong man? and then he will spoil his house (Matthew 12:29).

This verse can also apply to our house or family members and loved ones that he has held captive in the house of sin and death. We have the power over the devil and his demons to see our families and others saved from his deception and power.

What are some additional things we can do to see the promise of God fulfilled for our families and loved ones?

THE FIRST AND SECOND MIRACLE BLESSING: CLAIM THE PROMISE FOR YOUR FAMILY

The first and second miracles of Jesus offer a pattern of what we are to do when we get saved. Let's take a moment to see how these two miracles are connected. The first miracle occurred when Jesus turned water into wine (see John 2:1-11). The Bible records that His second miracle was the healing of a nobleman's son who had died and was brought to life again: *"This is again the second miracle that Jesus did, when He was come out of Judaea into Galilee"* (John 4:54).

This second miracle is significant to our discussion of household salvation, for when the nobleman's son was healed, *"...the father knew that it was at the same hour, in the which Jesus said unto him, Thy son liveth: and himself believed, and his whole house"* (John 4:53). How encouraging it is to realize that the second miracle Jesus performed in His earthly ministry resulted in an entire household believing!

Why did nobleman's whole house believe? Because the son of the house was raised from the dead. Notice that John 4 makes reference to both Jesus' first miracle and the second He was about to perform:

"So Jesus came again into Cana of Galilee, where He made the water wine. And there was a certain nobleman, whose son was sick at Capernaum" (John 4:46). These two miracles are mentioned together to show us the process from being saved to being empowered to reach others, including our households, with the Gospel. Remember His first miracle involved filling empty vessels, six in all, with water:

> And there were set there six waterpots of stone, after the manner of the purifying of the Jews, containing two or three firkins apiece. Jesus saith unto them, Fill the waterpots with water. And they filled them up to the brim (John 2:6-7).

It is interesting that there were six water pots to be filled because the number six represents humankind. In the Bible, the number six is often associated with humankind; for example, man was created on the sixth day of creation. I believe the filling of these six water pots prophetically represents man being saved by and through the Word of God. The Word of God is often compared to water in Scripture: *"That He might sanctify and cleanse it with the washing of water by the word"* (Eph. 5:26).

Once the water pots were filled to the brim, the next thing that happened was the transformation of water into wine: *"When the ruler of the feast had tasted the water that was made wine..."* (John 2:9). I view this as a picture of the transformation we experience by the power of the Gospel. We are translated, or transformed, from one condition to another. We go from darkness to light and from a life of sin to a new life, as a new creation, in Christ Jesus (see 2 Cor. 5:17).

Now once the water in the vessel turned to wine, it was to be drawn out and given to others: *"And he saith unto them, Draw out now, and bear unto the governor of the feast. And they bare it"* (John 2:8).

What does this represent? I believe it is a prophetic representation of new believers being filled with the Holy Spirit. Once they are filled, like the water pots, they are to pour their lives and the Gospel into others through the power of the anointing. This is what Jesus referred to when He said, *"He that believeth on me, as the scripture hath said, out of his belly shall flow rivers of living water,"* speaking of the power of the Holy Ghost (see John 7:37-39).

In summary, when we get saved as empty vessels through the water of the Word like Jesus' first miracle, we then need to be baptized or filled with His Spirit, like in Acts 2, and the next process in Jesus' first miracle. After we are saved and full of the Holy Ghost, we need to share it with others. This is where the second miracle of Jesus comes in—the healing of the young boy who was dying. The only one who could save him was Jesus! Isn't that true today? We are all lost and dying without the Lord, and it is only through Him that we can be raised to a new life again. Once this child came back to life, his salvation affected the whole family, and the whole family believed!

To me, this is why these two miracles are mentioned together; the miracles illustrate a process by which we are saved, filled, and empowered to pour our lives into others, especially our families. Simply put, once we are saved and become filled with the Spirit, we need to go and believe for our families to come alive also!

STAND FOR YOUR FAMILY

How do we take a spiritual stand for our families? The first place to start is by praying for them and asking the Lord to send people into their lives to share the Gospel with them. When you pray for your family members, something happens. Remember, your relationship with God is that spiritual seed that affects your family's salvation.

You are the key that helps to unlock the door of salvation for your family! This is what happened with Abraham. It was his covenant with God that acted as a key to save his nephew, Lot: *"And it came to pass, when God destroyed the cities of the plain, that **God remembered Abraham,** and sent Lot out of the midst of the overthrow..."* (Gen. 19:29).

Abraham's walk with God made a way for Lot to be "sent out" or saved! The Lord remembered Abraham and the covenant He made with him, saving Lot in addition. When you pray, God delivers your family! If God did this for Abraham, He will do it for you. Go ahead and ask God to remember you and save your family!

Here are a few things you can do to prepare your family for salvation:

- Come to a revelation of household salvation to build faith for your family.

- Pray for your family; call their names out to God for salvation. Bind the devil from deceiving them from coming to the truth.

- Make sure your heart is right concerning them; forgive them and speak righteously concerning them.

- Share the Gospel with them when the opportunity is right. Ask God for wisdom and the right opportunities.

- Show them acts of love, kindness, and a Christian lifestyle without hypocrisy.

- Pray for other Christians to come into their lives. Do your best to avoid arguments, confrontations, and endless debates, while striving to maintain a peaceful relationship with them.

- Live a life of righteousness, integrity, and responsibility that reveals the blessing of God in your life.

Are you ready to see them saved and enter into a life of salvation, one by one? God will remember you as He remembered Abraham and send your relatives out from a life that has held them captive to sin. It is your promise! Now keep believing on the Lord Jesus for your whole household to be saved! You will be glad you did, and so will they!

Chapter Six

JESUS' STRATEGY TO REACH PEOPLE

Therefore those who were scattered went everywhere

preaching the word (Acts 8:4 NKJV).

"Hold on to that door and don't let go!" I yelled as I drove down the Interstate in a van full of people I was bringing to church. The sliding side door of the church van had fallen off and was being held on by a few of the passengers. I was determined to get this vehicle back to the church as I drove on the busy road. "Whatever you do, don't drop it, and please don't fall out!" I told them. Some of my passengers were screaming while others were silent in wide-eyed disbelief as I continued on my journey. The longer we went, the harder it was for the young men to hold on to the rusted door.

I know you are probably wondering what I was thinking—and understandably so. I was barely an adult myself at the time and would never do such a thing today. Looking back, I realize this was not the best way to run a friendly outreach program—bringing people to church in a van with a broken side door! I know this story sounds crazy and unsafe, to say the least; I thank the Lord that no one was hurt. But the encouraging thing to glean from this potentially disastrous and dangerous story is how blessed my local church was with the new growth, converts, and outreach program we had started.

There were those of us who didn't feel it was solely the pastor's responsibility to figure out how to grow the church. I loved my pastor and the church, and I wasn't satisfied with empty chairs during services, or unsaved people being lost without God. So I was determined to do something about it. I started by witnessing on the streets and various places on my own. I did this until I could no longer fit people in the two-door Pontiac Firebird I was driving at the time. I was seeing so many people get saved that I had to have a better plan; I simply couldn't get them all to church in my car anymore.

"THEY BROUGHT"

The church was actually growing, and excitement was in the air because of the new converts getting saved on the streets and at church. The street ministry and evangelism outreach I was part of was having great success. Why was this so? For the same reason that Jesus' ministry grew and His fame went around Galilee: *"And Jesus returned in the power of the Spirit into Galilee: and there went out a fame of him through all the region round about"* (Luke 4:14). His ministry grew because of the power of God changing people's lives through His message, healings, and deliverance. Yet, this was only possible because of one important principle: people got involved in reaching out to others. Jesus did not minister in isolation; He trained His disciples. Furthermore, look at all the times mentioned in Scripture when people brought those who needed a touch from God to Jesus, or the disciples. The Bible says it was the *people* who brought to Jesus those who needed to be healed or delivered:

> *When the even was come,* **they brought** *unto him many that were possessed with devils...* (Matthew 8:16).

> *And, behold,* **they brought** *to him a man sick of the palsy, lying on a bed...* (Matthew 9:2).

> *...***they sent** *out into all that country round about, and* **brought** *unto him all that were diseased...* (Matthew 14:35-36).

And great multitudes came unto Him, **having with them** *those that were lame, blind, dumb, maimed, and many others, and cast them down at Jesus' feet...* (Matthew 15:30).

...and **they went forth**, *and preached every where, the Lord working with them, and confirming the word with signs following* (Mark 16:20).

Insomuch that **they brought forth** *the sick into the streets, and laid them on beds and couches...There came also a multitude out of the cities round about unto Jerusalem,* **bringing** *sick folks, and them which were vexed with unclean spirits: and they were healed every one* (Acts 5:15-16).

In all of these verses, people brought others to hear the message Jesus was preaching and to be healed or delivered. It was *"they"* who *"brought"*—not just Jesus or the disciples who spread the message. In other words, they took responsibility to bring people to Jesus!

This worked in the days of Jesus' ministry; it worked in the church I was attending; and it will work in our churches today to reach people. We must get a passion, a burden, and make it our responsibility to reach others and grow the churches we attend. This is the vital ingredient that is missing in many Christians' lives and churches: taking personal responsibility for sharing our faith and growing our churches. How crucial it is to recognize that sharing the Gospel is not the sole responsibility of pastors or leaders—it is ours as well.

No matter who we are, we can all reach out to others in the love of God and the power of the Gospel. This is what I did at the church I was attending. I would go minister to people and then bring them to church on Sunday. I had such a passion to win people. I started an inner city outreach in Omaha, Nebraska, where I lived at that time. So many people were getting saved that I could no longer pack them into my car or the church van, especially after the door came off. I would faithfully share my faith and bring people to church. I would literally pack them in.

Finally, I was able to use the church bus to bring all the people to whom I was ministering. I had never driven a bus before, yet faithfully week after week I drove that yellow piece of metal on wheels. I have so many unforgettable memories from that time: people singing, gang members carrying knives and guns on the bus until I confronted them, and sliding down an icy hill with no way to stop but by screaming the name of Jesus!

And then there was that unbelievable night when the silly bus, filled with people, caught on fire on the highway! Suddenly, smoke started filling the interior, and flames leapt out from under the hood. "Don't panic!" I hollered, to no avail. My passengers started to scream and panic, jumping out the back and front doors. They were yelling hysterically that the bus was going to blow up! It was utter panic as smoke poured out from the fire. Even after we had all exited the bus, many were so convinced the bus was still going to blow up, they started jumping over the guard rail, rolling down a hill onto the shoulder of another highway! The police and firemen finally showed up to bring order—thank God they did!

Now, my purpose for telling you these stories is that, hilarious and harrowing as these rides often were, if I hadn't been willing to go and reach out to others, they mostly likely wouldn't have come to church. Someone had to bring them. Like the people in Jesus' day, I had to be one of those who *brought*.

I was an ordinary young man who just wanted to make myself available to preach the Gospel and reach people. If God can use a guy like me, with no experience, then He can use anyone. We just have to be willing to be one of those who bring—making a difference in someone's life and helping him or her come to the Lord. This is a powerful strategy in reaching people, and the Lord Jesus understood the importance of having the right strategies.

THE JESUS STRATEGY

He knew the power of one particular strategy that reaches people with great results: the "Jesus Strategy"! While Jesus preached the kingdom, healed the sick, and cast out devils, there was one key thing He did that was really powerful in reaching people. I call it the power of ministering to your sphere of influence—His strategy for reaching people in a more effective way!

If you study the Gospels, you will notice that one of His methods of spreading the Gospel involved reaching people, touching their lives, and sending them back to their own personal sphere of influence. What did this look like? Most often, after someone received a touch from Jesus, He would either tell the person not to tell anyone, or He would send him back to his own personal sphere of influence.

In Mark 1, we read that Jesus told a leper after He healed him to tell no man:

> And saith unto him, See thou say nothing to any man: but go thy way, shew thyself to the priest, and offer for thy cleansing those things which Moses commanded, for a testimony unto them (Mark 1:44).

Why would He say such a thing to this man, especially after such a powerful miracle? I believe one reason was that He didn't want people to try to crown Him the natural king of Israel, missing His purpose for coming to the earth. However, this man could not keep quiet about his healing; and with great excitement, he told as many who would listen!

> *But he went out, and began to publish it much, and to blaze abroad the matter, insomuch that Jesus could no more openly enter into the city, but was without in desert places: and they came to him from every quarter* (Mark 1:45).

On another occasion, Jesus wouldn't let a man who was healed and delivered join His ministry team:

> *Now the man out of whom the devils were departed besought him that he might be with him: but Jesus sent him away, saying, Return to thine own house, and shew how great things God hath done unto thee...* (Luke 8:38-39).

The Lord told him to return to his own personal sphere of influence. He was to tell his family what the Lord had done. Why wouldn't the Lord let this excited man join His team? First, I believe the Lord knew he could be more effective in his own sphere of influence than by joining the crusade team at that moment. Second, Jesus wanted him, as we have been discovering in this book, to go reach his family immediately! Once again we see how much the Lord wants our families saved!

In this example, Jesus does the opposite of requesting silence about a miracle. He sends this man back into his own sphere of influence, starting with his family, and encourages him to let others know what God has done. This strategy worked because people were already waiting for Jesus to show up to meet their needs—all because one man couldn't keep his mouth shut! *"And it came to pass, that, when Jesus was returned, the people gladly received him: for they were all waiting for him"* (Luke 8:40). This proved to be an effective way of spreading the good news about Jesus and will work for us today as well. When our lives are transformed by His power, we can't keep silent! Perhaps this is why Paul said, *"For though I preach the gospel, I have nothing to glory of: for necessity is laid upon me; yea, **woe is unto me, if I preach not the gospel!"*** (1 Cor. 9:16).

Jesus knew that when people experience something life changing they want to share it. Jesus also knew that people always go back to their own sphere of influence to share great things that have happened. This was one of Jesus' strategies to spread the Gospel in a greater, more effective way. Once He ministered to their needs, He expected them to go tell somebody! After all, isn't that the Gospel? It is the good news that we can't be silent about. "The Jesus Strategy" encourages people to testify for themselves in their personal spheres of influence.

This is what happened when Jesus was ministering to the Samaritan woman at the well. After He ministered supernaturally to her, telling her detailed events of her life, she believed and told the whole city! *"Come, see a man, which told me all things that ever I did: is not this the Christ? Then they went out of the city, and came unto him"* (John 4:29-30). Jesus had a strategy, and so should we if we are going to be effective in reaching people with greater results.

I went out to reach people with the church van and bus I was using to minister the Gospel because I couldn't keep quiet; I had to tell somebody. Once people got saved, we worked very hard to get them connected to church and a discipleship program; then we encouraged them to go back into their own neighborhoods or spheres of influence. This was a more effective way to reach more people. We were using "The Jesus Strategy" and didn't even know it at the time!

Having the right strategies are important to winning the lost! The Bible even tells us to be wise and use wisdom in reaching people (see Prov. 11:30). I remember asking the Lord for wisdom and a strategy to reach people when a certain concert came to my city (my sphere of influence). This concert featured a popular band known for being very dark and occultic. I asked the Lord for a strategy, and He told me to go the night before the concert and pray. I was to pray mostly in the spirit, walking around the city auditorium seven times as I did so, without drawing attention from those around me. On the night of the concert, I was to minister the Gospel at the end of the event. God told me, "Minister at the end of the event so they won't think you are protesting the concert and will be more open to hear your words."

So, I did exactly what the Lord instructed, which included walking around that auditorium the night before seven times! Let me tell you, that was a lot of walking and praying. There were a few times I wanted to quit because of the effort involved. However, I am glad that I didn't. Do you know why? The night of the concert was amazing! I went there with some friends of mine, and after the event let out, the Lord told me that, as the people were coming out the doors of the auditorium, I was to stand on a ledge there and offer a free gift. *What free gift?* I thought. Again, the Lord had a strategy; I was shaking in nervousness. I opened my mouth and began to offer a free gift as the Lord told me. I yelled out, "Anyone want a free gift? Come over here if you want a free gift!"

My free gift was salvation, according to the Word that says, "The free gift of God is eternal life in Christ Jesus" (see Rom. 6:23). It was absolutely God what happened next! The people stopped, creating a jam at the door—and a crowd of hundreds gathered, listening to me offering the free gift of salvation through Jesus Christ!

Had we not had the right strategy of praying the night before and ministering after the concert, they may have thought we were protesting rather than reaching out with the Gospel. This is why it is vital to ask the Lord for wisdom and His strategy to reach people. I believe because we prayed and sought the Lord for His strategy, we got these great results!

REACHING YOUR SPHERE OF INFLUENCE

We can all agree how important it is to have effective methods to reach more people. This is why we must employ "The Jesus Strategy" and reach our sphere of influence. It is proven to be one of the most effective ways to minister the Gospel. Think for a moment of what you can do to be a blessing in someone else's life and also help your church to grow. A good place to start is to find people in your sphere of influence. You can do this by reaching those who you already know or see on a regular basis. These are people in your everyday life, neighborhood, job, or the places you frequent like the grocery store, the place you get coffee, or anywhere else.

Another thing you can start with, as we have learned from previous chapters, is your own family, or relatives. This is what Andrew, one of Jesus' disciples did. He went to his sphere of influence by reaching out to his brother Simon Peter, telling him about Jesus:

> One of the two which heard John speak, and followed him, was Andrew, Simon Peter's brother. He first findeth his own brother Simon, and saith unto him, We have found the Messias, which is, being interpreted, the Christ. And he **brought** him to Jesus... (John 1:40-42).

Notice the Scripture says that Andrew first went to a member of his family, his brother Simon Peter. Can you imagine for a moment what would have happened if Andrew hadn't told his brother? Peter may never have become one of the greatest apostles to lead the early church; his writings are still impacting generations today! Thank the Lord that Andrew *"brought him to Jesus"* (John 1:42).

Another person who reached their sphere of influence was Philip, a disciple who went and found his friend Nathanael:

> *Philip findeth Nathanael, and saith unto him, We have found him, of whom Moses in the law, and the prophets, did write, Jesus of Nazareth, the son of Joseph* (John 1:45).

The examples of Andrew and Philip should encourage us to reach our families, loved ones, and our broader sphere of influence for the Gospel.

- Start with your family, friends, or sphere of influence, as Andrew and Philip did (see John 1:41,45).

- Be willing to share your faith and the experience you have had with Jesus. This is what Andrew did; by telling his brother, he found the Messiah (see John 1:41). It is also what Philip did when he told Nathanael that he had met Jesus of Nazareth of whom the law and the prophets did write (see John 1:45).

- Invite them to meet the Lord by leading them in a salvation prayer, or invite them to church and special Christian events: *"And Nathanael said unto him, Can there any good thing come out of Nazareth? Philip saith unto him, Come and see"* (John 1:46).

- Be active in reaching out to the unsaved and sharing the Gospel by bringing them to the Lord, or by blessing them in some way that will open their hearts to the Gospel. Remember, they "brought" (see John 1:42). Philip brought Nathanael to Jesus by telling him to come and see.

The good thing about sharing the Gospel with those you know or meet regularly is that a form of trust is established. Furthermore, it is often easier to share the Gospel with someone we have talked to versus a complete stranger. I found this to be true when I brought co-workers to church after answering their questions about the things of God. I tried hard not to overdo it with the presentation of the Gospel. I made sure I worked hard and lived an upright life in front of them, never apologizing for my faith. Over time, I won their trust to be heard, and they would join me for church; some even gave their lives to the Lord.

Sometimes we may get an unpleasant or skeptical response. We shouldn't let that bother us; even Philip encountered some of that when he told Nathaniel he had met Jesus: *"Philip findeth Nathanael, and saith unto him, We have found him, of whom Moses in the law, and the prophets, did write, Jesus of Nazareth, the son of Joseph"* (John 1:45). Notice Nathanael's skeptical, even sarcastic reply: *"And Nathanael said unto him, Can there any good thing come out of Nazareth? Philip saith unto him, Come and see"* (John 1:46). I want to encourage you not to give up, even if, at first, the people you reach out to reject you or are skeptical. If they don't receive your message, just keep praying and asking the Lord to open their hearts. Philip didn't give up; he simply said, *"Come and see"* (John 1:46).

Not everyone we try to reach for the Gospel will accept or respond in the way we like.

- Some will believe: *"And some of them believed, and consorted with Paul and Silas; and of the devout Greeks a great multitude, and of the chief women not a few"* (Acts 17:4).

- Others will not believe: *"But the Jews which believed not, moved with envy...set all the city on an uproar"* (Acts 17:5).

- Some will be ready to receive after searching for the truth: *"...they received the word with all readiness of mind, and searched the scriptures daily, whether those things were so"* (Acts 17:11). This caused many in Berea to believe the Gospel they preached: *"Therefore many of them believed"* (Acts 17:12).

Generally speaking, when we minister the Gospel, there are usually three responses that we will receive. These can come from families, friends, loved ones, co-workers, neighbors, and all those to whom we speak about Jesus. These three responses include 1) those who believe and receive; 2) those who are skeptical and may or may not receive; and 3) those who don't receive. We find these examples when Paul was preaching in Athens on Mars Hill. They are found in Acts 17:32-34 and reveal these different responses to the Gospel:

- Some rejected the Gospel and mocked it: *"And when they heard of the resurrection of the dead, some mocked"* (Acts 17:32).

- Some were skeptical, needing to hear more information: *"...and others said, We will hear thee again of this matter"* (Acts 17:32).

- Some accepted the Gospel: *"Howbeit certain men clave unto him, and believed"* (Acts 17:34).

In spite of how people may respond to the Gospel, no one is without hope, and everyone must be given an opportunity to get saved.

THE THIEF WHO WENT TO HEAVEN

Even in the last moments of life, anyone can be saved! This is what happened to a thief being crucified next to Jesus on the cross. The Bible tells us of two thieves who were dying next to Jesus; one thief called out to the Lord to be saved, and the other mocked Him. In his final breaths, this thief found his salvation through Jesus. How did he do that, and what can we learn from his salvation experience?

The thief's road to salvation is also a pattern for leading someone to the Lord today (see Luke 23:39-43). It also reveals the Romans Road method that many use in evangelism.

- He expressed belief in a future life by stating that he feared God and was in the last moments of his life: *"But the other answering rebuked him, saying, Dost not thou fear God, seeing thou art in the same condemnation?"* (Luke 23:40). People need to be made aware that there is a future life after they die—of Heaven for the believer or hell for the unbeliever. They need to know God didn't come into this world to condemn them but to save them (see John 3:17).

- He acknowledged he was a sinner: *"And we indeed justly; for we receive the due reward of our deeds: but this man hath done nothing amiss"* (Luke 23:41). This is important when we are sharing the Gospel with a person; we have all sinned, and there is not one person who is righteous according to the Bible (see Rom. 3:10,23).

- He confessed with his mouth Jesus as Lord and believed God would raise Jesus from the dead: "*And he said unto Jesus, Lord, remember me when thou comest into thy kingdom*" (Luke 23:42). This thief did what Romans 10 says concerning salvation: we must confess with our mouths the Lord Jesus and believe in our hearts that God raised Him from the dead (see Rom. 10:9-10). He did this by calling Jesus Lord and asking Jesus to remember him when He came into His kingdom. In the same way, the unsaved people we are reaching need to understand who Jesus is, why He came, and that He died on a cross and was raised from the dead. They must also understand that salvation involves making Jesus Lord of their lives.

- He had faith that he would be forgiven of his sins because he had heard Jesus forgive: "*Then said Jesus, Father, forgive them; for they know not what they do*" (Luke 23:34). People need to be reminded that Jesus paid the price for their sins, forgiving them on the cross (see Rom. 5:8; 6:23). Those to whom we are reaching out must be given the opportunity to have their sins forgiven by the Lord.

- He believed that God the Father would raise Jesus from the dead, and he called upon the Lord to be saved: "*And he said unto Jesus, Lord, remember me when thou comest into thy kingdom*" (Luke 23:42). The people we are ministering to must believe God raised Jesus from the dead and that He is Lord. If they call upon the name of the Lord, they will be saved (see Rom. 10:13).

- He received the promise of eternal life: *"And Jesus said unto him, Verily I say unto thee, Today shalt thou be with me in paradise"* (Luke 23:43). We need to give people the opportunity to pray, asking Jesus to come into their hearts, forgive their sins, and be the Lord of their lives. When they do, they receive eternal life and need to be faithful daily to love, serve, and obey the Lord.

I once knew an older gentleman who asked me to come and pray with him. He was told by the doctors that he didn't have long to live. He was afraid of dying because he had done things he thought the Lord wouldn't forgive him for; he questioned if he was going to Heaven. Much like the thief on the cross, he had a moment with Jesus before his departure from earth. He repented privately in his heart for his sins as tears streamed down his face, and he committed his heart to the Lord afresh. I am convinced that, like the thief who went to Heaven and this gentleman, some people think they have done such wrong that they aren't worthy. They get into Heaven by the skin of their teeth, so to speak, by committing their lives to the Lord on their death beds.

If a thief could go to Heaven in his final moments in this life, even after all he had done, there is hope for the hardest, most sinful heart. The important thing is to try to reach these people before they slip into eternity without God. This story should remind all of us not only how short this life is, but also how vital it is to reach people. May it give hope to those who think the person they are trying to reach is too far gone, and to those who know someone they fear may have died without God. We don't often know what happens in the final moments of someone's life on earth if they haven't received the Lord. It is comforting to know that some may have called on the Lord to be saved in their final breaths!

THE NET AND THE POLE

If we are going to reach people and bring them to Jesus, there are two strategies that will help us accomplish this: the "pole" and the "net." Let's go back to the Gospels and think about fishing for a while. When Jesus selected certain of His disciples, He chose fishermen and asked them to follow Him while they were casting their nets (see Matt. 4:18-19). He told Simon Peter and Andrew that He would make them fishers of men: *"And he saith unto them, Follow me, and I will make you fishers of men"* (Matt. 4:19). He was speaking to men who were fishermen by trade; He was relating to their culture, speaking their language. He compared preaching the Gospel to fishing in the Sea of Galilee. We see this when Jesus was speaking to Peter after they had caught a net full of fish supernaturally by the Lord's blessing: *"And so was also James, and John, the sons of Zebedee, which were partners with Simon. And Jesus said unto Simon, Fear not; from henceforth thou shalt catch men"* (Luke 5:10). These disciples knew how to catch fish, but Jesus would now show them how to catch people with the Gospel.

Before we set out to do some spiritual fishing, we must pursue a heart-understanding of what the Lord identified as the greatest commandments. The first is to love God with our whole being so that His compassion can flow into the lives and needs of others (see Mark 12:29-31). The second is to love others and care for their needs as we would care for our own. This means we are to love people and reach them by showing them God's love! Jesus modeled these commandments to His disciples; they are the basis of all truly successful fishing expeditions.

In natural fishing, you can use a fishing pole or a net; these are two different methods by which to fish. In spiritual fishing, the same is true; we pull some from the grips of the devil and hell into the kingdom of Heaven by means of the "pole" and the "net."

A fishing pole usually catches one fish at a time. Ministering to that one person with the right strategy or bait is called the spiritual fishing pole method. With this method, you minister to people individually and may only reach a few in a day's work or at one time. A net, on the other hand, can gather more fish. When we use this method to gather in souls, we are usually dealing with larger numbers and venues. Churches with a strong evangelism thrust have the capacity to cast a wide net to gather in nonbelievers! Whether we are using the pole or net method, we need to know how to be effective.

Jesus used both of these methods to reach people with the Gospel. He used the fishing pole method when He was with people one on one: the woman at the well, the leper, the blind man, Nicodemus, and many others. When you use a fishing pole, you can bait the hook or put lure on the line and then cast it into the water to catch the fish. You have to have the right strategy or method if you are going to have success reaching different kinds of fish. The same is true if you are going to reach certain people for the Gospel.

At the church I pastor in Omaha, we decided it would be fun to have a men's fishing day at a nearby lake. This was an awesome time. We had some men who are fishing experts and could probably have had their own television shows. We had other men who only fished occasionally, being considered average fishermen. But one man stood out from all the others! The church I pastor is multicultural, and we had a gentleman who was from a particular tribe in Africa that might be considered very traditional, without modern technology or conveniences.

It was a beautiful night for fishing; the men were baiting their hooks and casting their fishing poles into the water. All of a sudden this man from Africa started hollering and ran full speed into the water with his pant legs rolled up; he tried to thrust his fishing pole into the water like a spear. The pole went into the water and vibrated; bending, it sent the man backward, shock written all over his face. You can imagine how everyone reacted! There was such a roar of laughter that no one, including him, could contain it. We had to kindly explain to him that the fishing pole wasn't a spear! We showed him the right strategy for fishing in this setting. You see, he was fishing according to his culture and preference—not understanding that in the United States fishing poles do not double as spears. He was using techniques that didn't work in his new culture.

This is why Paul said, "I become all things to all men" (see 1 Cor. 9:19-23). He didn't mean that he compromised spiritually or morally just to reach someone; he meant that he entered into their lives and culture in such a way that he could both connect with them and effectively share Christ with them.

Paul further explains that whatever we do must be for the glory of God (see 1 Cor. 10:31). We do this by following Jesus' example both in character and power, observing how He walked on this earth and how He dealt with people: *"Be ye followers of me, even as I also am of Christ"* (1 Cor. 11:1). Our number one priority is to represent Jesus, while understanding and seeking to minister to different people in their own cultures. We are to do this without sin or compromise. If we are going to have God's blessing and good results, then this is a key aspect of evangelism.

The Lord made another reference to the pole method when He told Peter to cast out for a very special fish:

> *However, so that we do not offend them, go to the sea and throw in a hook, and take the first fish that comes up; and when you open its mouth, you will find a shekel. Take that and give it to them for you and Me* (Matthew 17:27 NASB).

I believe Jesus wasn't just speaking of a natural coin (to pay a local tax), but of that one person who has something of value to give in this life that will benefit others. This includes everyone who is born in this world; in God's eyes, everyone has value and is worth catching for Him.

Jesus used the net method when He taught the crowds, healed them, delivered them, and fed them by multiplying the bread and fishes. We know from Scripture that beyond the twelve disciples the Lord had many followers—the seventy who were sent out to villages that Jesus would pass through; the women who followed Him and helped support Him; the crowds who were hungry for miracles, signs, and wonders. These broader categories of those who followed the Lord indicate that the net method was a necessary aspect of Jesus' ministry and bore much fruit.

Jesus instructed His disciples to go and reach humanity with His love and power. He gave them power to preach His Kingdom, heal the sick, and cast out devils. It is our responsibility to reach people. Whether we are using the spiritual pole or net method, we must be wise so we can get the right results.

Years ago, when I was still in high school, some friends and I went on a fishing trip. We were not experienced fishermen and didn't catch anything but a few little fish...and something else. We brought a guy on the trip with us who was more of a bookworm than an outdoors adventurer; he was considered to be one of the brainy kids at school. We didn't usually hang out together, but he offered to bring the food and cook for us, so it was too good of a bargain to pass up.

There was only one problem: he couldn't fish, and the thought of touching the bait was more than he could handle. We spent a long time trying to explain to him how to bait the hook and cast his fishing pole into the water. This didn't work very well for him because he kept snagging the trees all around him until he caught that "something else" I mentioned. He caught one of my friends right in the back with his fishing hook! He was oblivious to this and kept yanking on his fishing pole trying to get it unstuck, all the while digging the hook farther into my friend's back! My friend was screaming and looked like he was going into shock! It was not a small hook, and it required medical attention to get it out. I don't think we ever asked that guy to go fishing again.

Because he was unskilled and careless, he did more damage than good. Jesus doesn't mean for us to be careless either as fishers of men—snagging people, yanking them around, causing pain. We simply can't afford to be careless, reckless, or unskilled. I have written this book not only to stir a passion in you to reach others, especially your family, but also to give you helpful ideas for success.

In order to become skillful "fishers of men" as Jesus said, we must have the right bait to reach people. The right approach will win the hearts of those who don't know the Lord. Just as in real fishing, the right bait is essential for whatever fish you are trying to catch; otherwise, you may catch nothing at all. This has happened to me many times when I have gone fishing. I have walked away with only fish stories of all those "huge" fish that got away because I lacked the skill or used the wrong bait.

You also have to know your fishing ground. In spiritual fishing, we might call this your "sphere of influence." I once snagged some seaweed and trash when I went fishing and caught nothing the rest of the day because the place I had chosen wasn't conducive for catching fish. It was full of seaweed and junk, and fish weren't biting. After I changed my location and strategy, I had more success. Certain types of fish require certain bait and fishing strategies to get them to bite. This natural analogy implies that in spiritual fishing we also need to be wise in our methods and our approach.

Ask yourself some important questions: "What is my current sphere of influence?" "Where do I have favor?" "What are the key 'fishing grounds' in my life?" "Do I need to change my focus or my strategy?"

I used to say that fish never jump into the boat, referring to those who don't know the Lord. However, I actually did have a small fish jump into my boat once when I was fishing. I have also occasionally had a few unsaved people stumble into my church without anyone inviting them. They just jumped in like that fish into my boat, came to the church, and got saved without any "bait" or person witnessing to them. This, of course, is not the norm, but unfortunately, it has become the mindset of many pastors, churches, and Christians. We think if we have a beautiful building, great location, and the right programs, unsaved people will just jump right in, give their hearts to the Lord, and join the church. Sometimes we think that people will just jump into Heaven on their own initiative as well. This is lazy evangelism; rather than being active fishers of men—and training others to fish as well—we just wait for the "fish" to come to us.

This might happen from time to time, but it isn't the normal way of reaching people. Most people get saved through relationship. Someone has taken the time to tell them of Jesus through either the pole or net method:

> How then shall they call on him in whom they have not believed? and how shall they believe in him of whom they have not heard? and how shall they hear without a preacher? (Romans 10:14)

I want to encourage you to make an effort to reach all those within your sphere of influence for the Lord. You are part of the divine strategy of the Lord to bring people to Him! We have a purpose in this life, and that is to love Him and love those He loves. Let us help Him reach as many people with this love as we can. Let's take "The Jesus Strategy" and tell others what the Lord has done in our lives. Start with your family, friends, loved ones, relatives, co-workers, and those you meet in your everyday sphere of influence.

Are you ready to go fishing? Grab your net and fishing pole, and let's go!

Chapter Seven

LET'S GO!

And He said to them, "Go into all the world and preach

the gospel to every creature" (Mark 16:15 NKJV).

"Are you ready? Let's go!" said the leader of the witnessing team as we walked toward the auditorium. I was part of an evangelism team ministering in another city in front of their civic arena. My heart was pumping fast because I was nervous about what I was going to do; I had only been saved a couple of years and had been asked to carry a large cross in front of this event as the other team members handed out Gospel tracts. I shouldered the heavy cross and started walking toward a large crowd of people who were assembling for the weekend event. To me, everything felt surreal, like it was happening in slow motion. I wasn't prepared for what happened next.

People began to oppose my carrying a cross. They got angry— spitting on me, yelling in my face, pushing me, picking up the cross, and slamming it down on the cement. Others were taking aerosol cans, spraying them in the air, and then lighting the gas, hoping to scare or burn me. I was afraid, but at the same time I had a perfect peace because I could sense the presence of God upon me, protecting me. I remember thinking, *Why are these people so angry? I am just carrying a cross.* I hadn't been saved long enough to understand that people often respond to the Gospel with hatred, anger, and outright rebellion.

Such an experience shouldn't surprise us—not only did Jesus encounter such treatment when He carried His cross, so did the apostles and the early church. They were persecuted, stoned, and put to death for the Gospel they believed and preached. As a young Christian, however, I scarcely realized what kind of initiation that small command, "Let's go!" would bring.

Jesus originally gave that command—to His first disciples and to every disciple who has followed: *"And He said unto them, Go ye into all the world, and preach the gospel to every creature"* (Mark 16:15). Most of us don't fully understand the cost and commitment of such a command. First of all, it is not a suggestion; it is a command! Nor does it guarantee that everyone we minister to will be nice, respectful, and receive our message. On the contrary, we may face opposition, persecution, and hatred, which is meant to keep us from sharing our faith!

BECOMING THE HOUSE OF JASON

We must not forget that those who live godly lives in Christ Jesus and share the Gospel will suffer persecution! (See Second Timothy 3:12.) This shouldn't stop us because we have the answer through Jesus to touch and change the world.

"Let's go!" is my oldest son's favorite phrase when he is excited about something. He will yell, "Let's go!" loudly and passionately when he watches his favorite football team or when he heads out the door to something he enjoys. In the same way, Jesus is excited for souls to be reached and wants us to be passionate about it too! I believe this passion is the essence of His command to the disciples, "Go into all the world and preach the Gospel"; He wants us to have the same "Let's go!" attitude and action that perseveres in the face of opposition. I believe this attitude will develop as we, individual believers and churches, commit to a lifestyle of winning the lost. This attitude must permeate our mission to reach the unsaved.

As we determine to *go*, let's take a moment to consider three categories of people for whom every individual and church should specifically pray and reach. First, there are those who want more of God and His Spirit—like the house of Cornelius whose whole family was devout but not yet filled with the Holy Ghost (see Acts 10:1-2). They had never experienced the deeper things of the Spirit. Many people today are devout in this same way—going to church and living good Christian lives, but wanting and needing more of His Spirit.

Second, there are those who are devoted to their religion or its traditions but who haven't been born again. They are comfortable with their family's religious affiliation, beliefs, and traditions, but they haven't experienced the Lord on a personal level (see Acts 2:5).

Last, there are those who are heathens, bound by some false truth or belief. They form their own gods and ideologies, choosing to believe their own way or not at all (see Acts 17:16-18). Today we see people who worship idols, sports figures, movie stars, their own bodies, and many other things but don't give themselves wholeheartedly to the Lord. Just as in the book of Acts, some people today are pagans, idol worshipers, and atheists.

In the Bible, we find a family that represents this "Let's go" attitude and spirit so needed today. As we have been discovering, God values families and wants them saved. In the book of Acts, we read of one particular home that was definitely under attack from the devil—the house of Jason! Prophetically, this house is a model that we as the Body of Christ need to emulate. Understanding the significance of the house of Jason underscores how much the devil hates household salvation and people who preach the Gospel.

This was the case with a man named Jason and his household who came under assault by the religious leaders of Thessalonica and those who dwelt there. Jason's household was being attacked because they embraced Paul and Silas, an apostle and prophet, receiving them into their home:

> But some of the Jews were jealous, so they gathered some troublemakers from the marketplace to form a mob and start a riot. They attacked the home of Jason, searching for Paul and Silas so they could drag them out to the crowd... (Acts 17:5-6 NLT).

Satan hates effective apostles and prophets because their ministries bring spiritual breakthroughs and miracles; he does everything he can to hinder them. He also hates what the "House of Jason" prophetically represents. When we understand what this name prophetically represents, it will be easy to understand why this household was viciously attacked.

The Greek word for Jason is *Iasón.*[1] It means to heal, to cure, healing, including of physical disease. It is also from the verb *iaomai*, meaning to heal, cure, make whole.[2] In Hebrew, Jason is a derivative of the name Joshua, meaning salvation. So, we can see from these two definitions that the spiritual House of Jason has two key expressions: healing and salvation! We then can conclude prophetically that the spiritual expression of the House of Jason is healing and souls saved! That means any believer or church that sets out to heal the sick and win souls can be classified as being part of that spiritual house today.

This is why the devil, as he did in the book of Acts, attacks the spiritual House of Jason. He doesn't want any church or believer to win souls to Christ or operate in healing and miracles. We can't let that stop us as we remember that Jesus commissioned His disciples to win souls and heal the sick when He told them to preach the Gospel! (See Mark 16:15-18.) The Lord also wants churches to grow and become spiritual Houses of Jason where multitudes come to Him. Remember, it was the Lord who was adding to the church through the apostles (see Acts 2:47).

How does God reach people? He draws people by His Spirit. However, it all comes down to a divine partnership of human responsibility coupled with God's Spirit. In other words, God needs you and me to reach people. We see this, for example, where God was working with people in the great commission: *"And they went forth, and preached every where, the Lord working with them, and confirming the word with signs following"* (Mark 16:20).

This is how God added to the church in Acts. Notice it was God working together with believers! It started in the Upper Room with just 120, then grew to 3,000, 5,000, and whole multitudes. How did this growth happen? God worked with believers through salvation and healings just as the prophetic meaning of the House of Jason indicates.

When we set out to save souls and heal the sick as the spiritual House of Jason, then we will be able to reach people all around the world as the apostles did. We will reach:

- *Those in the earth*, just as Noah's house was saved from a global flood (see Heb. 11:7).

- *Those in our cities*, just as Rahab's house was saved in the city of Jericho (see Josh. 6:25).

- *Those in our families*, just as the jailer's whole house was saved (see Acts 16:31).

God is once again bringing out the prophetic significance of the House of Jason so we can reach our families, cities, and nations for God! As I've said, Satan knows this, so he attacks the House of Jason, using people, demons, and circumstances to try to stop healings, miracles, and souls from being saved. In Acts 17, the devil was so angry that Paul and Silas had come to this city that he stirred up many of the Jews to assault the House of Jason:

> *...They rushed to Jason's house in search of Paul and Silas in order to bring them out to the crowd. But when they did not find them, they dragged Jason and some other believers before the city officials, shouting: "These men who have caused trouble all over the world have now come here, and Jason has welcomed them into his house..."* (Acts 17:5-7 NIV).

This was no small uproar; the whole city and political officials were being affected according to this accusation: *"they trouble the city!"* (Acts 17:6). The devil was angry at Paul and Silas as well as the House of Jason because of all the healings, miracles, and salvations that were happening. The devil isn't threatened by a believer or church that isn't doing much, but when you add the dimension of God's power, healings, miracles, and salvation, then look out! He gets rattled every time!

On one occasion when I was ministering overseas in what was being advertised as a miracle conference, something caught my attention in one of the meetings. There were a few armed military soldiers at the back of the auditorium with guns in hand and stone-cold expressions! I finally decided to ask the host before I preached why these soldiers were standing in the back of the auditorium and attending this meeting.

The host replied, "They are here to make sure that what we advertised on the posters happens." I said, "You mean like signs, wonders, and miracles?" He replied, "Yes, that is right—and if we don't have what we advertised, they are going to shut down the meeting and will not let us meet in this auditorium anymore, guilty of false advertising!" I took a deep breath and walked to the platform, trying to reassure myself that everything would be fine. Thank God that He honors His Word! There were countless miracles happening everywhere as I ministered. The Lord healed the sick in such a powerful way! The soldiers were so deeply touched by God's power that they couldn't deny it was the Lord, and they didn't cancel the meeting.

This meeting could have been shut down and brought under persecution from the city officials, like the House of Jason in Acts 17. We must remember that as Christians and as the Body of Christ we need to keep ministering in the power of God and winning souls like the spiritual House of Jason. This will always bring glory to the Lord even though we may come under attack from the devil or other people.

It is obvious then why the devil attacks Christians who preach the Gospel and minister in the power of God. He wants to keep us weak and intimidated so we won't reach people. He doesn't want you to know that as a believer you have special rights and power to minister to people everywhere. Remember, Jesus gave us these believer's rights in Mark 16:15-20. Among many other things, He gave us the authority to cast out devils and heal the sick. The true expression of the Gospel is one of power that brings salvation! (See Romans 1:16.) This means we need to operate like the spiritual House of Jason and demonstrate the power of God through healings, miracles, signs and wonders!

"LET'S GO" REACH OUT AND TOUCH SOMEONE

It is one thing to know that we as believers have spiritual rights to minister in salvation and healings through the power of God. However, it is another thing to act upon those rights. The key thing is to always look for ways to reach out and touch someone! This is one of the most effective ways to put the "Let's go" commission into action. We can start with those who are closest to us first, such as family and friends, and then reach out to others—neighbors and co-workers—who may not be as close.

Reaching people on a one-on-one basis is a great place to start. Jesus did this from time to time: when He ministered to Nicodemus; the woman at the well; and the woman caught in adultery. His love and power turned people's hearts to Him. Even Philip the evangelist ministered to an Ethiopian eunuch one on one:

Later God's angel spoke to Philip: "At noon today I want you to walk over to that desolate road that goes from Jerusalem down to Gaza." He got up and went. He met an Ethiopian eunuch coming down the road..." (Acts 8:26-28 MSG).

The key is to find those in our lives with whom we have favor or have gained trust. When we have, pray and ask the Lord for an opportunity to share the Gospel and minister in the Lord's power, called the anointing. This is what Jesus did everywhere He went, preaching and demonstrating the power of God through the anointing of the Holy Spirit:

How God anointed Jesus of Nazareth with the Holy Ghost and with power: who went about doing good, and healing all that were oppressed of the devil; for God was with him (Acts 10:38).

And Jesus went about all the cities and villages, teaching in their synagogues, and preaching the gospel of the kingdom, and healing every sickness and every disease among the people (Matthew 9:35).

There was once a very influential person I was trying to reach with the Gospel. It seemed that nothing I did made that much of a dent because he already felt he was a good person, a religious person. However, when I would discuss having a personal relationship with the Lord, he didn't understand. So, I invited him to meet with my wife and me and asked if we could pray for him, and he agreed. As soon as we started praying, God's power and presence filled that room! He started shaking and couldn't remain standing because of the anointing of the Holy Spirit! When my wife and I opened our eyes, his eyes were big and his mouth wide open as he asked us what had just happened. He had felt electricity throughout his body, and he couldn't stand.

This is also what the Gospel is for—to demonstrate the Lord's power. When something stronger than what he was used to, God's presence, came upon him, it got his attention! This is what happened with Jesus; everywhere He went, people were being affected not only by His message but by the power of the Holy Spirit! *"And Jesus returned in the power of the Spirit into Galilee: and there went out a fame of him through all the region round about"* (Luke 4:14).

As Christians, we have not only the powerful Word of God but also the power of His Spirit to help meet the needs of people. I want to encourage you to ask the Holy Spirit to anoint you with His power and give you opportunities to minister the Gospel and demonstrate the Lord's power to someone in need.

One time I had a certain guy I worked with who wouldn't let me share my faith and told me to keep that "Jesus stuff" to myself. I would try to do kind things for him and testify of God's goodness in my life, but this man would have none of it! That all changed one day at work when he had been complaining for some time about having knee pain. On this particular day, he actually couldn't walk very far at all as he winced in pain. It took several co-workers to help him into a chair. What happened next I just couldn't believe! He yelled, "Hey, get over here and pray for my knee!"

I was shocked at what he asked, but I quickly ran over to pray for him. Just as I was going to pray, the devil planted a thought in my head: *What if he doesn't get healed?* I listened to that thought for about 30 seconds and then began to pray. When I finished, he said, "Wow, my legs are burning," and started to move his legs back and forth, bending his knees. God healed his knees, and he never complained thereafter. From that moment on, he was open to hearing, discussing, and asking questions regarding the Gospel!

My wife, Brenda, had something similar happen years ago when she had an opportunity to pray for her boss. Brenda was scheduled for a job review and was meeting with her unsaved boss privately in a meeting room. The boss began to tell my wife of all the problems that she was having in her life. My wife asked if she could pray for her. Her boss agreed; as Brenda prayed, the anointing began to touch her boss in a powerful and dramatic way. She started shaking and was visibly touched by the Lord; she told my wife that she had never felt that before. Again, it was the power of God that got her attention and opened her heart for the Gospel. After this event, my wife ministered the Word on a regular basis with her boss—all because of the power of the Holy Spirit!

When sharing our faith, we must remember the natural principle of seed time and harvest: *"While the earth remaineth, seedtime and harvest, and cold and heat, and summer and winter, and day and night shall not cease"* (Gen. 8:22). The same principle is true for winning people to the Lord. It takes first a "seed" spoken, revealed about Jesus or the Gospel to be planted in a heart, followed by some "time" for the Holy Spirit to convict of sin and work on that heart, until finally there is a "harvest" of salvation. This is why we need not be discouraged; sometimes we are expecting the harvest of salvation immediately to come, but do not forget that planting a seed of the Gospel is necessary in order to see the harvest of salvation.

On another occasion, I had been trying to share the Gospel with one gentleman all afternoon. Yet he kept getting more defiant, argumentative, and angry. I was becoming frustrated; I was about to lose my Christian testimony for a second and sock him one! Well, not really, but had it gone on any longer I might have at least thought about it. It wasn't until the Lord spoke to me that I understood. He said, "Hank, you are pouring it on so thick that you are muddying his heart rather than planting a seed. Let Me work on the words you plant. I want you to be finished now; leave him alone, and leave him to Me. But I want you to continue to pray for him to be saved."

We must remember that when we are dealing with someone who is not born again, a sinner without God, he or she is going to be convicted of sin and may react in different ways. Remember how Adam and Eve responded to God in the Garden after they had sinned? Those who are living in a sinful state without God today behave similarly when they come under spiritual conviction of sin. When Adam and Eve sinned, they tried to minimize their shame by covering it up and shifting the blame. We need to remember this when reaching out to touch someone for the Gospel.

- They tried to cover their sin and nakedness: "*...and they knew that they were naked; and they sewed fig leaves together, and made themselves aprons*" (Gen. 3:7). People today often do the same thing, trying to cover up their shame and their empty hearts with other things.

- They tried to hide from God and what they had done: "*And they heard the voice of the LORD God walking in the garden in the cool of the day: and Adam and his wife hid themselves from the presence of the LORD God amongst the trees of the garden*" (Gen. 3:8). This is often the reaction of people under the conviction of the Holy Spirit. Just like Adam and Eve, they run and hide from God, or anything that represents the Lord, while trying to live life on their own terms.

- They try to justify their actions and lifestyle: "*And he said, I heard thy voice in the garden, and I was afraid, because I was naked; and I hid myself*" (Gen. 3:10). Adam and Eve made excuses to justify their actions and their new lifestyle separate from God. In the same way, people will excuse their sinful behavior, trying to justify their actions or lifestyles. They will mention the way they were raised or things that have happened in their lives.

- They start to blame others to excuse their own behavior: "*And the man said, The woman whom thou gavest to be with me, she gave me of the tree, and I did eat. And the LORD God said unto the woman, What is this that thou hast done? And the woman said, The serpent beguiled me, and I did eat*" (Gen. 3:12-13). We are often like Adam and Eve when we are convicted of sin. We look for someone or something to blame to take the attention away from our sinful behavior or lifestyle.

There isn't just one method to reach people. It is most important that we pray, asking the Holy Spirit to speak and soften an unbeliever's heart. We should also ask the Lord to give us wisdom to know the best way to minister to each individual we encounter.

My wife, Brenda, and I were flying to minister together for a meeting when a man sitting next to us asked us what we did for a living. We explained to him that we were both in the ministry and Christians. He responded to us that he was a doctor and a devout Muslim. We began to talk back and forth about our faiths. He was trying to convince us of his Muslim faith, and we were telling him about Jesus and ministering the Gospel. He was very intellectual and had an answer for everything, even though his responses spoke in pointless circles. This discussion went on for some time as it was a long flight.

Quietly in her heart Brenda had been asking the Lord how to reach him during the conversation, and the Lord gave her a question to ask. She asked him to tell her why he was a Muslim in ten words or less. "What?" he asked, stumbling over his words and stall-ing. "You said ten words or less?" "Yes," my wife said, "and I can tell you in ten words or less why I am a Christian." He began to try to answer my wife's question and couldn't do it. He would start and then stop changing his answer numerous times. He was talking a bunch of theological jargon but not making sense. Finally, my wife interrupted by saying, "I can tell you in ten words why I am a Chris-tian...Jesus died for me, and no one else did that." That question and her answer changed everything as he looked shocked; it ended the discussion. Again, we must ask the Lord for the right methods to reach people. God is faithful to help us if we ask Him.

HOW TO REACH PEOPLE

First of all, we need to pray for a burden for people; we need to become compassionate toward those who don't know the Lord. Sec-ond, we need to be willing to be available to the Lord in reaching others. "How do we do that?" you might ask. By letting people see our Christian lives; by being witnesses of Christ to them and sharing our faith. This is what Jesus meant when He said that we are the light of the world; we shouldn't hide our faith or our Christian lifestyle (see Matt. 5:14-16). We must remember that we represent Jesus every time we go out in public and throughout our everyday life. Whether it is our family, job, talking with neighbors, or our daily routine, we must be alert for opportunities to share our faith and represent Jesus well. I once heard someone say that most people would rather *see* a sermon than *hear* one any day.

Here are some things you can consider when trying to reach someone for the Gospel:

- You can offer to pray for them. You can do this by look-ing for ways to bring healing spiritually, emotionally, and physically. This is what Jesus did; He brought healing to someone that He knew: *"When Jesus came to Peter's house he saw Peter's mother-in-law lying sick in bed with a fever. He touched her hand, and the fever left her; and she got up and waited on Him"* (Matt. 8:14-15 NIV).

- You can invite people for dinner or go to lunch with someone. *"While Jesus was having dinner at Matthew's house, many tax collectors and sinners came and ate with him and his disciples"* (Matt. 9:10 NIV). We can learn from this example that visiting the house of an unbeliever can bring opportunities to demonstrate the love of God.

- You can reach out to others in a nonthreatening way in their own environment. *"When one of the Pharisees invited Jesus to have dinner with him, he went to the Pharisee's house and reclined at the table"* (Luke 7:36-38 NIV). Jesus showed us that we need to relax and learn how to adjust to others' environments as long as it doesn't involve sin or compromise. Putting people at ease helps demonstrate true love and concern and sets an atmosphere for the Lord to move.

- You can invite them to church or a Christian event. Even the Holy Spirit is inviting people to be part of the Body of Christ: *"And the Spirit and the bride say, Come. And let him that heareth say, Come"* (Rev. 22:17).

There are many today who don't go to church but say they would visit if someone were to ask them. Why not ask someone you know to visit your church or Christian event? It's worth a try! Don't give up just because they may say no. Remember, some plant, some water, but God gets the increase (see 1 Cor. 3:5-8).

You might be thinking, *Well, what do I say to someone I am trying to reach with the Gospel?* You can always talk about the current topic being discussed or about the activities of the church. We all know people who aren't saved. Maybe they are unhappy with or feeling spiritually unfed in their current spiritual life or church. Perhaps they are bound by religion and looking for a place where the power of God is flowing. We don't have to preach a full sermon, but we can invite! We can all hand out a card, give a flyer, suggest a Website, or give out your pastor's book, tapes, or DVDs. Invite them to special events, conferences, or a special holiday service. The key thing is to be like Philip who invited Nathanael, telling him to come and see: *"And Nathanael said unto him, Can there any good thing come out of Nazareth? Philip saith unto him, Come and see"* (John 1:46).

My own salvation journey began with people handing out Gospel tracts that got me curious about the Gospel. Later, a high school friend invited me to his church, and I heard the Gospel preached, causing me to become convicted about my life without God. A few days later, I got saved while I was by myself in my bedroom.

Whichever method we feel led to use as we reach our families, friends, co-workers, or those we meet by "chance" throughout our day, it is vital to pray for opportunities and for specific people. We need to ask God to use us as well as others to reach the people who are in our lives.

Furthermore, we need to continue to be good students of the Word of God. We must know the Gospel message, the Scriptures, and what Jesus came to do. This is very helpful when coupled with our own testimony! The Bible tells us to always be ready to give an answer concerning the hope within us (see 1 Pet. 3:15).

I learned how important that was when I had a landlord who could never get my name right. He would call me five or six different names whenever he saw me, always forgetting which name was mine. He greeted me by saying, "Hello, Mike, Mick, Mack, Mark, Hank, Glen." Now these were some of the names of my roommates at the time, but he could never get mine right! He had a story for everything…if I mentioned the moon, he would say that, at one time, he was in line to be one of the first astronauts. If I mentioned the weather, he would say that he was once going to be a top weatherman for the weather channel! He was quite a character to say the least.

Yet, the one time I engaged him in a spiritual conversation, he asked me a question that I didn't have the answer for, as I had been saved only a short while at the time. When I finally had an opportunity to share Jesus, I couldn't give an answer because I didn't know my Bible! Neither had I rehearsed who Jesus was in my heart nor did I understand the power of sharing my testimony to lead someone to the Lord. Had I known, it would have been a great way to bypass a slew of theological questions that often result in endless debates and arguments.

As you prepare yourself to lead others to Jesus, start simply with prayer—asking God for His compassion and love. Ask the Holy Spirit to anoint you with wisdom, power, and boldness, followed by opportunities to share your faith and display His power. Once you step out to talk about the Lord with someone, relax; don't feel like you have to start with heavy revelation or convince the individual immediately. It is helpful to establish some kind of common ground with those you are trying to reach. This helps to break down suspicion and can also help you overcome your apprehension.

THE PRAYER FROM THE CRYPT

THE APOSTLE PAUL'S WAY OF REACHING PEOPLE

Let's take a moment to learn from the apostle Paul as he preached the Gospel and testified of his salvation experience before King Agrippa. We find this example in Acts 26.

- *Be willing to speak about your salvation.* The first thing we note about Paul is that he was bold and unashamed to share his faith: *"Then Agrippa said unto Paul, Thou art permitted to speak for thyself. Then Paul stretched forth the hand, and answered for himself"* (Acts 26:1).

- *Be joyful in your salvation.* Paul showed joy and was happy about his Christianity: *"I think myself happy, king Agrippa, because I shall answer for myself this day before thee touching all the things whereof I am accused of the Jews"* (Acts 26:2). People who are always depressed, unhappy, or wear their problems and feelings on their sleeves are not as convincing in their walk with God as those who try to maintain joy in their salvation.

- *Be willing to share your experience of what led you to the Lord.* Paul gave a clear testimony before the king: *"My manner of life from my youth, which was at the first among mine own nation at Jerusalem, know all the Jews; which knew me from the beginning, if they would testify, that after the most straitest sect of our religion I lived a Pharisee. And now I stand and am judged for the hope of the promise made of God, unto our fathers..."* (Acts 26:4-23). You do this by sharing your testimony (see Acts 26:12-17). This is because it is good to share what Jesus has personally done for you. This is especially helpful if someone wants to argue doctrine, or wants to know if Adam had a belly button, or if there is life on planet Zeta, for example. Instead, testify of your new life in the Lord and how your life was different before you started walking with Him. This is helpful because although people may want to argue Bible facts, your experience is difficult to contest. Try not to dwell on your past or glorify it. It is important only for the purpose of showing the difference "before Christ" and "after" you started walking with Him.

- **Minister the Gospel and the importance of turning your life to God.** *"Whereupon, O king Agrippa, I was not disobedient unto the heavenly vision: But shewed first unto them of Damascus, and at Jerusalem, and throughout all the coasts of Judaea, and then to the Gentiles, that they should repent and turn to God, and do works meet for repentance..."* (Acts 26:19-23). It is important to tell what God has done for you and share the message of salvation. The apostle Paul shared what it really means to be a Christian and shared the Gospel and talked of repentance.

- **Don't let persecution and opposition stop you from sharing the Gospel.** *"As he thus spake for himself, Festus said with a loud voice, Paul, thou art beside thyself; much learning doth make thee mad"* (Acts 26:24). Paul defended himself and certainly let them know he wasn't crazy—that his life had truly been touched by the Lord. *"But he said, I am not mad, most noble Festus; but speak forth the words of truth and soberness"* (Acts 26:25).

The methods that the apostle Paul used to share his faith were almost enough to convince the king to be saved: *"Then Agrippa said unto Paul, Almost thou persuadest me to be a Christian"* (Acts 26:28). All Paul had to do was be willing to be bold and plant a spiritual seed in the king's heart. We can apply these same principles Paul used when sharing our faith. If it worked for him, it will for us!

NOW LET'S GO!

We are just about at the end of this book; my hope is that you have learned much and are ready to reach as many people as you can for the Lord. I am praying that the "Let's go" burden for the lost is becoming stronger in you.

There are two things I want to suggest that will help in continuing your commitment to reach your family and others for the Lord as we bring this book to a close. They are two questions that we find in Scripture that aid us in reaching others. They are two questions that give us clues to reaching our families and loved ones: 1) What is in your house? and 2) What is in your hand? While both of these questions are similar, they each offer different things that people have available in reaching people for the Gospel.

What do I mean by "What's in your house?" I am referring to things we have in our own homes, or lives, that through acts of kindness can open the door to speak to others about Jesus. Jesus fed the multitudes because meeting their needs or being kind opened the door of their hearts to receive the Lord. We each possess many earthly and spiritual things that can bless others. What it takes is the realization that we have been blessed in order to be a blessing. If we look at our lives and homes, we would be surprised at the things we have that can really bless someone else.

Making an impact in someone else's life is such a rewarding feeling. If you were to think for just a moment, I bet you would find that you have something in your house and hand that can be a blessing to someone. This is what we find in Second Kings 4 when the prophet Elijah asks a widow woman an important question: *"And Elisha said unto her, What shall I do for thee? tell me, what hast thou in the house?"* (2 Kings 4:2).

Her reply reveals that she didn't think she had anything in her house or life of any significance. She tells Elisha that she has nothing in her house except a pot of oil. Sound familiar? We all do this same thing at some time or another by thinking we aren't significant or don't have anything that will really be a blessing to others. We often say such things as, "I don't have any value in my life," or "I only have a few dollars," or "I don't own much," or "I'm not good at this or that." What this woman didn't realize was just how much the oil in her home would prove to be a blessing!

In the same way, we all have something the Lord can use to bless someone else. We may not think it is important or of any value, but God does. He can use what we have if we are willing to give it or to go and bless someone else with the Gospel. The oil in the woman's house prophetically represented the oil of the Holy Spirit, called the anointing or the power of God, and it is available to minister in the lives of others. *"And she said, Thine handmaid hath not any thing in the house, save a pot of oil"* (2 Kings 4:2). We have the power of God inside us that is available to others also. This woman had oil in her house, and we have the anointing oil of the Holy Spirit in us.

This oil or power is not as effective if we just hold on to it or keep it shut up inside us or the four walls of the church! This is why the prophet Elisha told this woman to go and get empty vessels and fill them with oil:

Then he said, Go, borrow thee vessels abroad of all thy neighbours, even empty vessels; borrow not a few. And when thou art come in, thou shalt shut the door upon thee and upon thy sons, and shalt pour out into all those vessels, and thou shalt set aside that which is full (2 Kings 4:3-4).

Just as she was to take the oil out of her house and pour into empty vessels, we are to do the same concerning the Gospel. Sounds just like the great commission to "Let's go," doesn't it? We are to take the anointing oil of the Holy Spirit inside us and share it with others, especially those whose lives are empty and without God.

This story presents us with a prophetic picture of the condition of many people today. They feel empty or hopeless without Jesus, like those empty vessels, and the only answer is for someone to be willing to take what they have in their house and share with them. This involves taking the power of God through the Holy Spirit into their lives.

This example of the woman and Elisha not only refers to God's provision but also to His salvation, including that of the household. The answer to these empty vessels is Jesus and His anointing. But in order for that to happen, someone must be willing to pour his or her life into them like this oil into the empty vessels. Notice the widow was to take the oil and pour it into the empty vessels she had borrowed from her neighbors. Prophetically, I believe this means that we are to look everywhere possible for a vessel to pour into, including our families, our neighbors.

We should never assume any vessel is beyond hope or reach. I believe this example of the woman and the empty vessels prophetically includes household salvations. The empty vessels might represent our families that are brought home and filled with oil:

And Elisha said, "Borrow as many empty jars as you can from your friends and neighbors. Then go into your house with your sons and shut the door behind you..." (2 Kings 4:3-4 NLT).

We need to be willing and available to give our lives for empty vessels. When we do, the anointing oil of the Holy Spirit upon our lives will touch and fill them. The Bible says that the vessels were filled. In other words, they were ministered to and discipled, causing the presence of God or the anointing to stay. All of this occurred by means of something that seemed so insignificant: a little pot of oil that filled empty vessels with oil.

And it came to pass, when the vessels were full, that she said unto her son, Bring me yet a vessel. And he said unto her, There is not a vessel more. And the oil stayed (2 Kings 4:6).

So, what do you have in your house and in your life that God can anoint to be a blessing to someone else?

One of the things that I do personally is remind myself that I have the power of the Holy Spirit inside me to reach others. I continue to fill myself with His Word, His presence, and commit to a life of fellowship and prayer with the Lord. Out of that lifestyle, I am ready to minister to those who need salvation or a touch from God.

I also look around my house for practical ways I can be a blessing to others. For example, I will often use my snow blower in winter to clear my neighbors' driveways as a way of showing kindness. Kindness often opens people's hearts and gives you opportunities not only to glorify the Lord but to share your faith. Gifts or acts of kindness have proven to be very valuable ways in winning someone to the

Lord: *"Everyone is a friend of a person who gives gifts!"* (Prov. 19:6 NLT). But true kindness has no ulterior motives. Love is the goal.

The second question is similar to the first question we asked ourselves. What is in our hands? In other words, what are some things we can do or some items we possess that can be a blessing to someone? This is what God asked Moses when he didn't think he had anything significant in his ability or power to help someone else. *"And the LORD said unto him, What is that in thine hand? And he said, A rod"* (Exod. 4:2). Moses didn't think it was anything but a shepherd's rod, but God thought otherwise. When Moses let go of it and let God use it, it became something powerful. *"And he said, Cast it on the ground. And he cast it on the ground, and it became a serpent; and Moses fled from before it"* (Exod. 4:3). Moses' rod turned into a snake! Through this rod God would deliver Israel and drown Pharaoh and his army. In other words, what Moses had in his hand was touched by the power of God to be a blessing to others. In the same way, we all have something that we can do, something we possess, or some talent we have that can be transformed by God's power if we give it to Him to bless others.

Let me share my own example of how God used what I had on hand to bless others. I had been traveling by plane and was sitting next to a young man who only spoke Spanish. I had tried to communicate with this man and share the Gospel, yet nothing was working until I gave him a children's book I had written that had been translated into Spanish. It opened the door to his heart. He began to read it quietly page by page. After he had finished reading it, I noticed a small tear falling from his right eye, and he smiled. I asked him if he understood, "Comprende?" He shook his head yes. I showed him the prayer of salvation at the end of this short book. He folded his hands and gave his heart to the Lord!

I used what I had in my hand. If a small children's book can touch a man, leading him to accept the Lord, what do you have available to reach someone? It doesn't have to be sophisticated or complicated—just something that can touch the heart of the one you are reaching.

It's as simple as, "What's in your house? What is in your hand?" Think for a moment about those questions. What do you have in your house and hand? Once you have the answer, step out and let your life be a witness.

We must not delay; it's time to reach people now before they are lost forever, pleading for someone to talk with their family, friends, and loved ones like the man in hell who cried out to no avail. We must decide that the time has come for us to go! Or should I say, *"Let's GO!"*

ENDNOTES

1. *Iasón*; see http://concordances.org/greek/2394.htm.

2. *Iaomai*; see http://concordances.org/greek/2390.htm.

AUTHOR CONTACT INFORMATION

Hank Kunnemann
5351 S. 139th Plaza
Omaha, NE 68137
USA

Phone: 402-896-6692

Fax: 402-894-9068

Visit Hank and Brenda Kunneman at their
Website: www.hankandbrenda.org

For more information about Hank and Brenda Kunneman, *One Voice* Ministries, or to receive a product list for books and audios or for information on speaking engagements, please visit www.hankandbrenda.org or write to One Voice Ministries.